D0923270

BURT FRANKLIN: BIBLIOGRAPHY AND REFERENCE SERIES #183

FIRST EDITIONS

OF

JAMES RUSSELL
LOWELL

A BIBLIOGRAPHY

OF THE FIRST EDITIONS IN BOOK FORM
OF THE WRITINGS OF

JAMES RUSSELL LOWELL

COMPILED LARGELY FROM
THE COLLECTION FORMED BY THE LATE

JACOB CHESTER CHAMBERLAIN

WITH ASSISTANCE FROM HIS NOTES
AND MEMORANDA BY

LUTHER S. LIVINGSTON

BURT FRANKLIN: BIBLIOGRAPHY AND REFERENCE SERIES #183

BURT FRANKLIN
NEW YORK

Published By
BURT FRANKLIN
235 East 44th St.
New York, N.Y. 10017

ORIGINALLY PUBLISHED
NEW YORK: 1914
Reprinted 1968

Printed in U.S.A.

TO THE MEMORY OF

JACOB CHESTER CHAMBERLAIN
WHO UNCONSCIOUSLY ERECTED
THIS MEMORIAL TO HIMSELF
THESE BIBLIOGRAPHIES
ARE DEDICATED
A.M.I.C.

PREFACE

THIS Bibliography of the First Editions of the writings of James Russell Lowell has been prepared upon the same plan as the Longfellow Bibliography published in 1908. It is a collector's bibliography and in its pages are described only first editions of Lowell's own books, pamphlets and leaflets, and first editions of other books, pamphlets or leaflets which contain, for the first time printed *in a book,* some writing of his. Magazines and periodicals, with the exception of a few of special interest to book-collectors, have not been described. Some volumes which contain a single letter of Lowell's and which, under the plan, should have been described fully, are simply mentioned and the location of the letter given. The list of books containing contributions of a more important character is long enough, though the Lowell specialist will want to secure every book containing a line of his writing. The catalogues of the auctioneers and dealers in autographs include many letters by Lowell, sometimes printed in full, but such publications have been ignored.

The arrangement is chronological by date of publication. As many books published in the later months of the year are post dated, those consulting the book may be sometimes misled. But in the Check List, following this Preface, the titles are arranged according to the printed dates upon the title-pages themselves and alphabetically by title, under the year.

The sizes given are according to the measurements adopted by the American Library Association and do not indicate the actual folding of the sheets. Blank pages are, generally, not mentioned in the collations. Page numbers in square brackets indicate only that the pages are unnumbered. Where the first and last of a series are in brackets there are often numbered pages between.

This volume is issued as the second of the "Chamberlain Bibliographies," though it might, with justice, be called the third of the series, the Catalogue of the exhibition of Hawthorne's books published by The Grolier Club in 1904 being the first. That Catalogue, which was compiled by Mr. Chamberlain, was practically a bibliography of first editions of Hawthorne, though it was less comprehensive in its scope than the Longfellow and Lowell bibliographies. In addition to the regular issue of the Exhibition Catalogue printed and distributed to the Club members, Mr. Chamberlain printed, for private distribution, forty copies on fine paper, with wide margins and bound in boards. This special edition contained some corrections and additions to the text, besides an Index and photogravure reproductions of two portraits.

Owing to a large number of letters from Longfellow to George W. Greene acquired by Mr. Chamberlain and freely quoted from in the Longfellow Bibliography, that volume contains a greater number of heretofore unpublished letters than does the present compilation. All of the letters printed here in full are believed to be hitherto unpublished. The shorter extracts, quoted because they throw light upon the publication of various books, are mainly taken from the published letters. The extracts from Briggs's letters to Lowell referring to "A Fable for Critics" are, mainly at least, here first published.

At the end of the Longfellow Bibliography there were printed a few poems which, probably through oversight, had not been reprinted by Longfellow during his lifetime or by his editors after his death. A much greater number of uncollected or dis-

PREFACE

carded poems by Lowell exists, enough to make by themselves a volume equal in size to the Bibliography.

The frontispiece to the present volume is a photogravure made from the life-size portrait in oils painted in London by Francis Lathrop, about 1884. The painting is now the property of The Grolier Club of New York (a gift from Mr. Beverly Chew), and this reproduction is made by the permission of the Council. Every lover of the writings of James Russell Lowell will, I am sure, join with me in thanking them for this privilege.

I am indebted to Mr. William Coolidge Lane for the photograph of the leaflet "All Saints" in Harvard University Library, and to Mr. Andrew Keogh for the photograph of the "Christmas Carol" leaflet in the Aldis collection in Yale University Library. Mr. William Bunker has permitted me to reproduce the Watertown broadside of 1842 from his copy. The other leaflets are reproduced from Mr. Stephen H. Wakeman's copies. Especial acknowledgment is due to Mr. Wakeman for numerous favors.

All of us who remember Mr. Chamberlain's interest, activity, enthusiasm and success in his chosen field of book-collecting will regret that time was not spared him to perfect and complete his collection of first editions of Lowell's writings, and to prepare his own Catalogue or Bibliography. To Mrs. Chamberlain's generosity is due the publication of this memorial of his interest in authors and books and book-collecting.

L. S. L.

CHECK LIST

CHECK LIST

CHECK LIST

CHECK LIST

CHECK LIST

CHECK LIST

CHECK LIST

This list is arranged chronologically by the dates upon the printed title-pages and alphabetically under the year. The arrangement in the text is the actual order of issue so far as can now be ascertained.

The titles with an asterisk prefixed are of books and pamphlets of minor importance, generally containing a single letter only. Though mentioned in the text they are not fully described, and are there always placed after the more important publications of the same year.

FIRST EDITIONS OF
JAMES RUSSELL LOWELL

1838

Harvardiana. | Volume IV. | [vignette and quotations] | Cambridge: | Published by John Owen. | M DCCC XXXVIII.

8vo. Collation: Title, imprint, Preface, and Index, pp. [i]–viii; text, pp. [1]–392. Size of leaf, untrimmed, 9⅝ by 5⅞ inches.

Issued in ten monthly numbers for September, 1837, to July, 1838, each number enclosed in a printed cover. The title and the preliminary pages were issued with No. 10.

Although the scheme of our compilation excludes periodicals, this volume of *Harvardiana* is described because it includes James Russell Lowell's first literary compositions, or at least the first which achieved the permanence of types. He was one of the editors whose names are signed to the Preface, which is dated "Cambridge, July, 1838." His associates were Nathan Hale, Jr., Rufus King, George W. Lippitt, and Charles W. Scates. As to the number printed, Edward Everett Hale says: "I do not think they ever printed three hundred copies. I do not think they ever had two hundred and fifty subscribers."

The following list of Lowell's contributions to the magazine is from the Appendix to Scudder's "James Russell Lowell, a Biography." The articles in verse are so indicated, the other pieces are in prose.

No. I. September, 1837.
  "Imitation of Burns." In verse.
  "Dramatic Sketch." In verse.
  "New Poem of Homer."
No. II. October, 1837.
  "A Voice from the Tombs."
  "What is it?" In verse.
  "Hints to Theme Writers."

"Obituary."
"The Serenade." In verse.
"The Old Bell."
No. III. November, 1837.
  "The Idler. I."
  "Saratoga Lake." In verse.
  "Hints to Reviewers."
  "Skillygoliana, I."

No. IV. January, 1838.
"Scenes from an Unpublished Drama, by the late G. A. Slimton, Esq." In verse.
"Skillygoliàna, II." In verse.
No. V. February, 1838.
"Chapters from the Life of Philomelus Prig."
"Skillygoliana, III." In verse.
No. VI. March, 1838.
"The Idler. II."
No. VII. April, 1838.
"Skillygoliana, IV."

No. VIII. May, 1838.
"A Dead Letter." In verse.
No. IX. June, 1838.
[Extracts from a Hasty Pudding Poem.] In verse.
"Translations from Uhland. i. Das Ständchen; ii. Der Weisse Hirsch." In verse.
No. X. July, 1838.
"To Mount Washington, on a second visit." In verse.
"Song: A Pair of black Eyes." In verse.

1838

To the Class of '38, | By their ostracized Poet, (so called,) | J. R. L. | [rule].

8vo. A single leaf, printed on one side only. The above is the heading. The poem, in two columns, separated by a vertical double rule, fills the lower four fifths of the page.

A half-tone reproduction (reduced in size) is in Edward Everett Hale's "James Russell Lowell and his Friends," Boston, 1899. There is no mention of the poem or of the reproduction in the text, but in the list of illustrations is the note: "From a printed copy lent by Mrs. Elizabeth Scates Beck, Germantown, Pa." I have been unable to see an original.

It seems probable that this leaflet was distributed to members of the Class at the Valedictory Exercises held July 17, 1838. The poem has not been included in any of the collected editions.

1838

Class Poem. | "Some said, John, print it; others said, Not so: | Some said, It might do good; others said, "No." | Bunyan. | M DCCC XXXVIII.

8vo. Collation: Title, imprint, Dedication, and Preface. pp. [i–v]; text and Notes, pp. [7]–52. Size of leaf, trimmed, 8¾ by 5⁷⁄₁₆ inches.

[4]

Issued in paper cover, the first page printed from the types of the title-page.

On account of unseemly behavior at chapel exercises, Lowell was, on June 25, "suspended till the Saturday before Commencement." He was sent to Concord, Mass., and put in charge of the Rev. Barzillai Frost, to whom he was to recite twice a day, and was "not to visit Cambridge during the period of his suspension." The printed programme of the Valedictory Exercises, held July 17, has as No. 4, "Poem by J. R. Lowell," but a foot-note says: "On account of the absence of the Poet the Poem will be omitted."

On August 9 he was "in doubt whether to have my 'Poem' printed or no." On the 17th he wrote: "The first eight pages of the 'Poem' are prob-ably printed by this time, and the proof on its winding way." This proof of the first eight pages was received by him the next day, though the poem itself was not yet finished. It was probably completed within a few days, as the printed poem is dated at end, "Concord, Mass., August 21, 1838." The Preface is dated "Concord, Mass., August, 1838." The Dedication reads: "To the Class of 1838, | Some of whom he loves, none of whom he hates | This 'Poem' is Dedicated | by | Their Classmate."

The pamphlet was probably printed before Commencement Day, which that year fell on August 29. The number printed must have been consid-erable, as it not infrequently comes into the market. The poem itself was never reprinted by the author.

A portion of the original manuscript of the "Class Poem," being pp. 4 to 13, with three interpolated pages and nine pages of Notes, was acquired by the late Edwin B. Holden. It is dated on the last page, "Concord August 15, 1838. | Wednesday Evg. | J. R. L." Below this are two draw-ings of faces in profile.

The following eight lines of verse, not a part of the poem, are on the last page and are here reprinted by the kind permission of Mrs. Holden:

"That man 's a most egregious poet
And wears long hair that folks may know it.
'T is true his verses do not show it
But what of that? He must be poet.
Is n't his hair twelve inches long?
Why 't is proof positive of song
Don't he feed Pegasus on clover?
Nay, don't he turn his dicky over?"

1841

A | Year's Life. | By | James Russell Lowell. | Ich habe gelebt und geliebet. | Boston: | C. C. Little and J. Brown. | [rule] | M DCCC XLI.

12mo. Collation: Half-title, title, copyright (dated 1841) and imprint, Dedication, and Contents, pp. [i]–viii; half-title and text, pp. [1]–182. A blank leaf at end is part of the last signature. Size of leaf, untrimmed, 7³⁄₁₆ by 4⅝ inches.

Issued in gray boards, with paper label, "A | Year's | Life."

Most copies have a slip of "Errata," seven lines, inserted facing p. 182. A few early copies were sent out before the error was discovered. A slip was then printed and lightly tipped in, in the copies already bound. In the case of the unbound copies the slip was pasted upon the last signature before binding. Mr. Chamberlain's copy, formerly Mr. Beverly Chew's (who secured it in England), and now Mr. Wakeman's, was of the earliest form, without errata slip. It has this inscription on the fly-leaf: "To | Alfred Tennyson | from the Author | Boston U. S." This volume may have been the beginning of a correspondence between the two poets. At least in December, 1841, Lowell was writing to Evert A. Duyckinck of a new and enlarged edition of Tennyson's poems which Moxon was about to publish, and says:

"I do not wish you to state your authority for this—but you may depend on it, for my authority is the poet himself. I have the great satisfaction of thinking that the publication is in some measure owing to myself, for it was by my means that he was written to about it, and he says that 'his American friends' are the chief cause of his reprinting."

The book was issued in January, 1841. An untrimmed copy (apparently the printer's press-room copy) has a pencil date, seeming to indicate the date of printing of the sheet, on the first page of each signature. Signatures 1 and 2 have "Jany 1"; signatures 3, 4 and 5, "Jany 7"; signatures 6 and 7, "Jany 9"; signatures 8 and 9, "Jany 12"; signatures 10 and 11, "Jany 18"; and signature 12 (the last), "Jany 19." Sometime between the latter date and the end of the month the book seems to have been bound.

On February 18 Lowell wrote: "My book, as you must know, is out. It has been received with distinguished favor, but as yet only two hundred and twenty five copies have sold." On March 15 three hundred copies had been sold, and he was writing of the prospects for a second edition, which, however, was never issued. Just how many copies were printed does not seem to be recorded. Lowell said that he "sent but a bare half-dozen to the press," as he despised the "system of literary puffing."

Edward Everett Hale prints a letter, from which the following is an extract, which shows that the author's ideas originally were very modest: "Now, if you will find out how much it would cost to print 400 copies (if you think I could sell so many; if not 300) in decent style (150 pages—less if printed closely), like Jones Very's book, for instance, I could find out if I could get an indorser. I should not charge less than $1 per vol.—should you? I don't care so much for the style of printing as to get it printed in any way." One friend (J. F. Heath), according to Mr. Scudder, "engaged to secure the sale of at least a hundred copies."

The volume contains thirty-three poems and songs and thirty-five sonnets, besides a dedication in verse, a prefatory poem without title, and a final one headed simply, "L'Envoi." Seven poems and two sonnets are all that are included in later collected editions.

The author's manuscript of "A Year's Life" is in the Morgan library. The manuscript proper consists of pp. 1–59, 60 and 61, 62–73, 73½, 74–90, written on one side of the paper only, with one leaf, written on both sides, inserted between pp. 74 and 75.

Three pieces are marked out in the manuscript and do not appear in the printed book:

"The Lover's drinksong." Pp. 14, 15 of the manuscript.
"Song. Something on the leaf is written." P. 5.
"Song. Thou giv'st me flowers." P. 31.

Accompanying the volume, and now forming a part of it, is a sheet, two leaves, of blue paper having on p. 1 the sonnet "To Keats," and on p. 4 the verses written to Maria White on her birthday—

"Maiden, when such a soul as thine is born."

This latter was first printed, with some alterations, in "Poems," 1844, and is included in the current editions. "To Keats" was printed in the *Boston Miscellany* for January, 1842, but seems never to have been reprinted.

Laid in the manuscript is the following autograph letter relating evidently to "A Year's Life" addressed to J. Frank Heath:

"Dear Ph.

"Where have you been these three days?

"I went into town yesterday—saw Little & settled all about the volume which will therefore soon go to press.

"J. R. L.

"P.S. I am sick—if you come back come and see me."

The letter is undated, but is indorsed "Wednesday Dec."

1841

The Token | and | Atlantic Souvenir, | an Offering | For Christmas and the New Year. | [waved rule] | Boston: | Published by David H. Williams. | Philadelphia, Thomas, Cowperthwaite & Co., Henry Perkins; New | York, Collins, Keese & Co.; Baltimore, Cushing & Brothers; | Cincinnati, U. P. James; St. Louis, J. C. Dennies | & Co.; London, Wiley & Putnam; Paris, | Jules Renouard. | [waved rule] | 1842.

[7]

ORDER OF SERVICES

AT THE

DEDICATION OF THE NEW CHURCH,

ERECTED BY THE

CONGREGATIONAL SOCIETY, IN WATERTOWN,

August 3, 1842.

---

1. ANTHEM.

"I will extol thee, O God, my King; I will bless thy name forever and ever," &c.

2. INTRODUCTORY PRAYER, BY REV. JOSEPH FIELD, D. D.

3. SELECTIONS FROM THE SCRIPTURES, BY REV. G. F. SIMMONS.

4. ORIGINAL HYMN, BY JAMES R. LOWELL, ESQ.

ONE house, our God, we give to thee:
One day in seven, Eternity
Floods all our souls, and in our eyes
Some thanks for thy great goodness rise.

Let us not think thy presence falls
Only within these narrow walls,
Nor that this handiwork of clods
Can prison up the God of gods.

Let us not think that only here
Thy being to our own is near;
But let us find thee every day
Forth in the fields, or by the way.

The world too many homes doth own,
Shall God the Father have but one?
Shall we his loving presence seek,
But one poor day of all the week?

O, let us feel thee every where
As common as the blessed air,
Among our neighbors and our friends,
The shaper of our rough hewn ends.

Here let us only need to meet,
Because our service is more sweet
When many hearts as one adore,
And feel thee through each other more.

Thy presence here we then shall seek,
As but an emblem of the week;
Secure that thou wilt bless us when
We strive to bless our fellow men.

Then shall this house indeed be thine,
A visible and outward sign
Of that unseen, encircling love,
Which doth in all our spirits move.

5. DEDICATORY PRAYER, BY REV. SAMUEL RIPLEY.

6. ANTHEM.

"Lift up your heads, eternal gates, unfold to entertain the King of glory," &c.

7. SERMON, BY REV. CONVERS FRANCIS, D. D.

8. HYMN, No. 529, Greenwood's Collection.

9. CONCLUDING PRAYER, BY REV. CALEB STETSON.

10. ANTHEM.

"Blessed be thou, Lord God of Israel, our Father, forever and ever," &c.

11. BENEDICTION.

J. Howe, Printer, No. 39, Merchants Row, Boston.

[REDUCED IN SIZE]

[8]

16mo. Collation: Title, copyright (dated 1841), note by Editor and imprint, Preface, Contents, and Embellishments, pp. [i–viii]; text, pp. [9]–320. Frontispiece, engraved title, and plates facing pp. 49, 91, 109, 141, 179, 219, 267, 295. Size of leaf, trimmed, 6⅝ by 4¼ inches.

Issued in stamped morocco, gilt edges, back lettered "The | Token | 1842."

This, the first annual to which Lowell contributed, contains "The Ballad of the Stranger. | By J. R. Lowell." Pp. 133–137. On February 18, 1841, the poet wrote to George B. Loring: "I have already been asked to write for an annual to be published in Boston," and, a month later: "I have just finished something which I ought to have done long ago. I have copied off a ballad of mine for a publisher of the name of D. H. Williams, who is getting out an annual. He will pay me five dollars per page, and more if the book sells well."

The poem was never collected or reprinted by the author.

1841

The Liberty Bell. | By | Friends of Freedom. | [quotation, 6 lines] | Boston: | Massachusetts Anti-Slavery Fair. | M DCCC XLII.

16mo. Collation: Title, imprint, and Contents, pp. [iii]–vi; text, pp. 1–204. Frontispiece, facing title; Lowell's sonnet engraved and printed on glazed paper, facing p. 152. Size of leaf, trimmed, 6⅝ by 4¼ inches.

Issued in yellow boards, gilt edges, front cover printed from the types of the title, but enclosed within a frame of a single rule.

This volume contains three sonnets by Lowell. Two are printed with the text, "Sonnets. | By James Russell Lowell." Pp. 37, 38. These are
I. "Great truths are portions of the Soul of Man."
II. "If ye have not the one great lesson learned."
The second was apparently never reprinted by the author.
The third sonnet is printed on a leaf of glazed paper, and inserted facing p. 152. It has the heading, "Pierpont. | Sonnet. | By James Russell Lowell." It was reprinted in "Poems, 1844," as "The Fiery Trial," but has never been collected.

1842

Order of Services | at the | Dedication of the New Church, | Erected by the | Congregational Society, in Watertown, | August 3, 1842.

8vo. A single leaf, printed on one side only. The above is the heading, followed by order of services, numbered 1 to 11. The fourth item is "4. Original Hymn, by James R. Lowell, Esq." with the hymn, beginning "One house, Our God, we give to thee:", eight stanzas of four lines each, printed in two columns. The whole is enclosed in wide ornamental border built up of floriated rhomboids, with corner rosettes.

Size of type-page, 8⁵⁄₁₆ by 6⅛ inches.

In the copy seen the eighth item, "8. Hymn, No. 529, Greenwood's Collection.", has the number altered in pencil to 531.

At this time Lowell was frequently visiting at the house of Abijah White, in Watertown, having first gone there as a guest of his son W. A. White, a college classmate of Lowell's. Here, in 1839, he met Maria White, to whom he was married in December, 1844. Professor Norton prints a letter of Lowell's in which he gives an account of a temperance celebration at Watertown, in July, 1842. It was quite in the order of events that he should have written a hymn for this church dedication, though the fact seems not to have been recorded by his biographers and the hymn itself has never been reprinted.

The only copy of the sheet which I have been able to trace is in the collection of Mr. William Bunker.

1842

The | Liberty Bell. | By | Friends of Freedom. | [quotation, 6 lines] | Boston: | Massachusetts Anti-Slavery Fair. | MDCCCXLIII.

12mo. Collation: Half-title, poem, title, imprint, and Contents, pp. [i]–viii; text, pp. 1–208. Portrait of Charles Follen facing p. [iii]. Size of leaf, trimmed, 7½ by 4⅝ inches.

Issued in yellow glazed boards, gilt edges, front cover printed from the types of the title, within a frame of a single rule with ornamental corners. Also issued in cloth, gilt edges.

This volume contains: "Elegy on the Death of Dr. Channing. | By J. R. Lowell." Dated at end "Boston, November, 1842." Pp. 12-17.

1843

The Pioneer. | A | Literary and Critical Magazine. | J. R. Lowell and R. Carter, | Editors and Proprietors. | [rule] | January, 1843. | [rule] | Vol. I.—No. I. | [quotation from Bacon, two lines] | [rule] | Boston: | Leland and Whiting, | 67 Washington Street, Opposite the Post Office. | [Then below the double rule border] Three sheet periodical. Printed by Freeman and Bolles. $3. per ann. in adv.

8vo. Collation: No title-page, above being the first page of the cover of the first number. No. I consists of text, pp. [1]–48, with heading "The Pioneer. | January, 1843." at top of p. [1]. With two plates, separately printed, "Circe" and "Two hundred years ago." No. II consists of text, pp. [49]–96, with heading "The Pioneer. | February, 1843." at top of p. [49]. With three plates "Genevieve," "Dante and Beatrice meeting," and "Dante and Virgil entering the dark wood." No. III consists of text, pp. [97]–144, with heading "The Pioneer. | March, 1843." at top of p. [97]. With two plates separately printed, "Dickens and the Artist in Boots," and "Orestes supplicating Apollo for purification."

Each number was issued in a paper cover of which the first page is the title. The second page of the cover of No. I is a "Prospectus | of the Pioneer," signed "Leland & Whiting" and dated "Boston, 1843." P. 3 contains an advertisement of Sparks's "Life of George Washington," and p. 4 contains "Embellishments," "Table of Contents," etc., with heading "The Pioneer. | January, 1843." P. 2 of the cover of No. II has a series of press notices of the first number, with heading "The Publishers of the

FIRST EDITIONS OF LOWELL

Pioneer respectfully call attention to the following notices | of the first number of their magazine, | ". These notices are continued on p. 3 of cover. P. 4 is "Embellishments" and "Table of Contents," with heading "The Pioneer. | February, 1843." Cover pages 2, 3 of No. III are blank. P. 4 is "Embellishments" and "Table of Contents," with heading "The Pioneer. | March, 1843."

The three numbers of this short-lived periodical are so closely identified with Lowell and are so coveted by collectors that they are here included and described thus fully.

Lowell had been a contributor to *The Boston Miscellany of Literature and Fashion,* of·which twelve numbers were issued from January to December, 1842, under the editorship of Nathan Hale. He was evidently planning this journal of literature (but *not* of fashion) as early as September 20, 1842, when he wrote to George B. Loring: "Nor am I at liberty yet to tell you my plan of literary support. If I could see you, I would tell it you by word of mouth, but I cannot bring myself to write it down." The prospectus of *The Pioneer,* dated October 15, 1842, though signed by the publishers, Leland and Whiting, was probably written by Lowell. Lowell and his associate Robert Carter were actually the proprietors as well as the editors. Their contract with Leland and Whiting bound them to furnish five thousand copies of each number by the twentieth of the month, under penalty of a fine of five hundred dollars. The third number was eight days late and the publishers demanded the forfeit but offered to waive it if the contract should be altered as to the number of copies they were obliged to take.

The publishers' circular "To Periodical Agents," in which they offered six copies of each number for one dollar, thirteen copies for two dollars, and so on up to one hundred and forty copies of each number for twenty-five dollars, is a desirable addition to a set of *The Pioneer;* as would be also, if a copy has survived, one of the hand-bills "in red and black, with a spread eagle at the head of them" which, Lowell wrote from New York, faced him everywhere.

The temporary loss by Lowell of his eyesight was, no doubt, the immediate cause of the suspension of *The Pioneer.* It is, however, very doubtful if, aside from this difficulty, it could have lasted much longer.

On March 24, 1843, Lowell wrote to Edgar Allan Poe:

"The magazine was started on my own responsibility, & I relied on the payments I should receive from my publishers to keep me even with my creditors until the Magazine should be firmly established. You may conceive my distress when the very first note given me by my publishers has been protested for nonpayment, and the magazine ruined. For I was unable to go on any farther, having already incurred a debt of $1,800 or more."

He had previously (on November 19, 1842) written to Poe: "If the magazine fail, I shall consider myself personally responsible to all my creditors."

Extant letters throw some light on Lowell's business methods and the relative value put upon contributions of various writers. To Poe he wrote: "I can offer you $10. for every article at first with the understanding that, as soon as I am able I shall pay you more according to my opinion of your deserts." To Whittier he wrote: "I cannot promise to pay you very much at first, for the expense of getting up such a work makes large holes in small capitals. But I trust that the hope of aiding a good endeavor will be enough to you." To John S. Dwight he wrote: "At first I shall not be able to pay as much as I wish. But I will give at the least $10. for every article of 3 pages or more & $2 a page for less. The possibility of raising our people's taste in this divine matter [music] must be a part of your reward at first. If the magazine succeeds I shall be able & glad to pay you as you deserve."

After the demise of *The Pioneer,* Poe wrote to Lowell, asking him to help him obtain an article from Hawthorne for publication in his new magazine, *The Stylus,* and saying that he would pay whatever Lowell paid Hawthorne.

On April 17, 1843, Lowell wrote: "Hawthorne writes me that he shall be able to send an article in the course of a week or two. His terms are $5. a page, but probably, as your pages will 'eat up' Copy with a less anaconda-like appetite than the fine print magazines, your best plan would be to pay him so much by the article."

Lowell's own contributions to *The Pioneer* are as follows:

No. I. January, 1843.
"Introduction."
"Voltaire."
"The Follower."
"Sonnet. Our love is not a fading earthly flower."
"The Plays of Thomas Middleton."
"The Rose."
Reviews of Dickens's "American Notes for General Circulation,"
and Hawthorne's "Historical Tales for Youth."
No. II. February, 1843.
"Song Writing."
"To M. O. S."
Reviews of "The Book of British Ballads," Longfellow's "Poems on Slavery," and Macaulay's "Lays of Ancient Rome."
No. III. March, 1843.
"The Street."

1843

The Gift: | A Christmas and New Year's | Present. | MDCCCXLIV. | [rule] | Philadelphia: | Carey and Hart. | 1844.

8vo. Collation: Title, copyright (dated 1843) and imprint, Contents, and List of Plates, pp. [i–v] ; text, pp. [7]–296. Frontis-

POEMS

BY

JAMES RUSSELL LOWELL.

———

CAMBRIDGE:

PUBLISHED BY JOHN OWEN.

M DCCC XLIV.

[SIZE OF ORIGINAL]

[14]

piece, engraved title, and plates facing pp. 44, 96, 139, 184, 221, and 255. Size of leaf, trimmed, 8⁹⁄₁₆ by 5½ inches.

Issued in stamped leather, back lettered "The | Gift | 1844."

This volume contains "A Requiem. | By J. R. Lowell." Pp. 37, 38. It is included in the volume of "Poems" published in December, 1843. This annual must have been published before October 6, 1843, as Charles F. Briggs refers to it in a letter of that date.

1843

The | Liberty Bell. | By | Friends of Freedom. | [quotation, 6 lines] | Boston : | Massachusetts Anti-Slavery Fair. | MDCCCXLIV.

12mo. Collation : Half-title, title, imprint, and Contents, pp. [i]–viii ; text, pp. 1–232. Portrait of Lucretia Mott facing title. Size of leaf, trimmed, 7½ by 4⅝ inches.

Issued in yellow glazed boards, front cover printed from the types of the title-page but within a frame of a single rule, with ornamental corners.

This annual contains "A Chippewa Legend. | By James Russell Lowell." Dated at end "Cambridge, October, 1843." Pp. 17–29. It was also included in the "Poems" published late in December, 1843.

Another annual, "Friendship's Offering and Winter's Wreath," Boston, 1843, contains, on pp. 121, 122, "Serenade. | By James Russell Lowell." This had been included in "A Year's Life," published in 1841.

1843

Poems | By | James Russell Lowell. | [rule] | Cambridge : | Published by John Owen. | M DCCC XLIV.

12mo. Collation : Half-title, title, copyright (dated 1843) and imprint, Dedication, and Contents, pp. [i]–xii ; half-title and text, pp. [1]–279. Size of leaf, untrimmed, 7¹⁄₁₆ by 4¾ inches.

Issued in boards, with paper label, "Lowell's | Poems | 1844."

A few copies were printed on large paper. Size of leaf, untrimmed, 10¾₆ by 6⅝ inches. These seem to have been mostly bound in boards, leather back, but I have seen one copy in paper boards, with a small fragment of a label remaining.

On September 19, 1843, Lowell wrote: "I am in treaty with Owen to publish a volume for me. He is a little afraid of the 'speculation,' but is very desirous to publish it, and will probably do so." The Dedication to William Page is dated at end, "Cambridge, December 15, 1843," and the book was published just at the end of the month. The copy sent to Charles F. Briggs contains an inscription dated January 1, 1844. Its receipt was acknowledged on January 6, 1844, and four days later Briggs wrote: "Your book is neither advertised nor noticed in the New York prints. You must speak to your publisher about it. I have seen it in some of the book stores and on several book tables. It is a thousand pities that you could not have got it here before Christmas. It would have helped the sale of some hundreds."

Mr. Chamberlain, by a study of broken and imperfect types in the two books, came to the conclusion that the large-paper copies were printed after the ordinary copies had been run off. This is the more usual custom. The number of special copies on large paper must have been very small; eight or ten copies only can now be traced.

On March 6, Lowell wrote to Briggs: "My Poems will soon reach a third edition of five hundred. About eleven hundred have thus far been sold, I believe." The second edition, printed from the same types as the first, differs from it only in having the words "Second Edition" on the title-page and in having the date "1841" added on p. 105. The third edition is identical with the second except for the words "Third Edition" on the title-page. Some copies of this third edition were issued in lithographed paper covers. Editions were issued in London by three different publishers during 1844. The one which we may suppose was the authorized edition, published by C. E. Mudie, is a page-for-page reprint of the first edition, with an added leaf of "Advertisement to the English Edition," following the title-page.

1844

The | Liberty Minstrel | [vignette] | [quotation, 1(lines] | [rule] | By | Geo. W. Clark. | [waved rule] New York: | Leavitt & Alden, 7 Cornhill, Boston Saxton & Miles, 205 | Broadway, N. Y.: Myroi Finch, 120 Nassau St., N. Y.: | Jackson & Chaplin 38 Dean St., Albany, N. Y.: | Jackson & Chaplin

Corner Genessee and | Main St., Utica, N. Y. | [rule] | 1844.

16mo. Collation: Title, copyright (dated 1844) and imprint, and Preface, pp. [i]–iv; text and music, pp. [5]–184; Index, pp. [185–187]. Size of leaf, trimmed, 6⁹⁄₁₆ by 4³⁄₁₆ inches.

Issued in cloth, lettered on front cover "The | Liberty Minstrel | by | Geo. W. Clark." It has no back lettering.

This song-book contains one poem never acknowledged and never collected: "Rouse up, New England. | Words by a Yankee. Music by G. W. C." Pp. 70–72. This had been published anonymously in the *Boston Courier* of March 19, 1844, and was, at the time, ascribed to Whittier. Mr. Pickard, in his Life of Whittier, Vol. I, p. 297, states that it was by Lowell.

On pp. 126, 127 is "Are ye truly Free? | Words by J. R. Lowell." This had been included in the "Poems" published the preceding December, under the title "Stanzas of Freedom," and, under this title, is included in later editions.

1844

The | Liberty Bell. | By | Friends of Freedom. | [quotation, 4 lines] | Boston: | Massachusetts Anti-Slavery Fair. | MDCCCXLV.

12mo. Collation: Half-title, title, imprint, and Contents, pp. [i]–vi; blank, pp. [vii, viii]; text, pp. [1]–256. Portrait of Wendell Phillips facing title-page. Size of leaf, trimmed, 7⅝ by 4⅝ inches.

Issued in yellow glazed boards, gilt edges, the first page printed from the types of the title-page; also issued in stamped cloth, gilt top.

This volume contains "The Happy Martyrdom. | By James Russell Lowell." Pp. 147–150. This poem was never collected or reprinted.

"The Odd-Fellow's Gem," Providence, 1845, but copyrighted and published late in 1844, contains on pp. 114, 115, "The Fatherland" by Lowell. This poem had, however, already appeared in "Poems," published in December, 1843.

1845

Conversations | on Some of | The Old Poets. | By | James Russell Lowell. | [waved rule] | [quotation, 5 lines] | [ornament] | Cambridge: | Published by John Owen. | M DCCC XLV.

12mo. Collation: Title, copyright (dated 1844) and imprint, Dedication, quotation (7 lines), and To the Reader, pp. [i]–viii; text, pp. 1–263. Size of leaf, trimmed, 7 by 4⅝ inches.

Issued in lithographed paper covers. Front cover lettered "Lowell's | Conversations. | Published by John Owen, Cambridge.", and on back, "1845 | Lowell's Conversations."

Although Mr. Cooke and Mr. Greenslet both state that this volume was published in December, 1844, I believe they are in error. On December 12, Miss White wrote to Charles F. Briggs: "James is so hurried with his book that he has not an instant to spare, and has therefore commissioned me to answer your letter, and account to you for his long silence. The truth is, he delayed writing his articles on Poets and Old Dramatists, or rather delayed arranging them in the form of conversations, until he had only two months left for what really required four. The book must be out before we are married; he has three printers hard upon for copy, for he has to rise early and sit up late, so that he can only spare time to see me twice a week, and then I have but transient glimpses of his dear face."

Lowell and Maria White were married on December 26, but the book was not ready for a week or two later. They left almost immediately for Philadelphia, where Lowell had been promised editorial work on the *Pennsylvania Freeman,* then just revived under the management of C. C. Burleigh and J. Miller McKim.

Mr. Hale's "James Russell Lowell and His Friends" contains a facsimile of the "List of Copies of the Conversations" to be given away by "The Don," and this list is printed by Mr. Scudder in an Appendix. It is undated, but was evidently drawn up before the book was published and just before Lowell's marriage and departure from Cambridge. The list gives twenty copies, of which No. 2 was to be sent to Charles F. Briggs. On January 6, Briggs wrote: "What has become of your Book? I have heard nothing about it." And on January 11: "I have received my copy of the 'Conversations' and have read it through with exceeding great pleasure. I hear it well spoken of on every hand. It is a thousand pities that it could not have reached here before Christmas, for it would have put a good many shillings into your pocket."

Nos. 11, 12 and 13 were to be sent to Lowell himself, "Through Anti-slavery office Care J. M. McKim." On January 14, in writing to Carter he said: "Give my kind remembrances to Austin and to Owen. The package of the latter came safe." On the next day, January 15, he gave away two copies of the book. One, afterwards acquired by Mr. Chamberlain, has Lowell's autograph inscription, "To Charles J. Peterson | With the affectionate regards | of J. R. L. | Philadelphia Jany 15, 1845." Peterson was the editor of *Graham's Magazine*. Another copy, given to Lydia Maria Child on the same day, is now owned by Dr. James B. Clemens. It has this inscription, in Lowell's autograph: "Mrs Child | With the affectionate regards of | James & Maria Lowell. | Jany 15, 1845." The seventeen copies, numbered 1 to 10 and 14 to 20 were to be sent direct from the publishers, and the presentation inscriptions, if Lowell's instructions were followed, were in the autograph of Robert Carter.

Besides these twenty copies, which were all the "author's copies" of the first edition which he was entitled to receive, he gave away a few others. One very interesting copy recently sold with the Browning library contained this inscription: "To Elizabeth B. Barrett, with the best wishes and heartiest congratulations of the author, Cambridge, Massachusetts, U. S. A. Feby. 1845."

The agreement with Owen for the publication of the book is as follows:

"Conversations on some of the Old Poets.

"The copyright of the above entitled book belongs to the Author James R. Lowell. John Owen the publisher has the sole right of publishing the work for three years from this date on condition of paying the Author on the day of publication ten cents for every copy printed & ten copies for every five hundred copies printed

"J. R. LOWELL.
"JNO. OWEN

On March 21, Lowell wrote to Briggs: "You will be glad to hear that the first edition of my 'Conversations' (1000) are gone already. I begin to feel rich. Owen owes me nearly $300. at this moment." Part of this sum must have been due him from the "Poems," as under the above agreement $100 would have been his royalty on a thousand copies.

The lithographed cover, printed in red, green, and gold, was from a design by Miss White. There are slight variations in the covers of different copies. In the majority of copies the words "Lowell's Conversations" are printed in green, but in a copy bound in stiff boards, covered with lithographed paper which is not turned under, these words are printed in gilt. This copy belonged to J. E. Cabot and was probably given to him by Lowell. Some copies have a series of gilt dots around the ornaments in the white spaces in the four corners of the front cover, while others are without these dots. I have also seen a copy printed in red and gold only. One copy examined has the date 1846 in green below "Lowell's Conversations" on the front cover, and is without the date 1845 on the back, but this cover, without much doubt, was prepared for the second edition, though used on some unsold copies of the first edition.

1845

Liberty Chimes. | [quotation, 9 lines] | Providence. | Ladies' Anti-Slavery Society. | 1845.

16mo. Collation: Half-title, title, imprint, and Contents, pp. [1–6]; blank, pp. [7, 8]; text, pp. [13]–148. Size of leaf, trimmed, 6¹¹⁄₁₆ by 4⁹⁄₁₆ inches.

Issued in boards, leather back, with paper label, "Liberty Chimes."

The volume contains "The Contrast. | By James Russell Lowell." Pp. 70, 71. It was afterwards reprinted as "A Contrast."

1845

[Lines On Reading of the Capture of Certain Fugitive Slaves near Washington. Boston, 1845.]

8vo. 2 leaves, paged 33–36. P. 33 begins: "(No. 9.) Read and circulate. | [Cut of a hand, with S S] | Walker resided in Florida with his family from 1836 until 1841. He | [etc., 14 lines in prose] | The Branded Hand. | By John G. Whittier"; at the top of p. 35: "Lines, | By James Russell Lowell, | On reading of the Capture of Certain Fugitive Slaves near Washington."; at bottom of p. 36, an advertisement of the "Anti-Slavery Fair." Size of leaf, trimmed, 8⅛ by 5¼ inches.

This poem first appeared in the *Boston Courier* for July 19, 1845. It was again printed in *The Liberator* for July 25, 1845, and was collected in the 1848 volume of "Poems." Mr. Chamberlain noted typographical differences between his copy and one in Harvard University Library.

1845

The | Liberty Bell. | By | Friends of Freedom. | [quotation, 4 lines] | Boston: | Massachusetts Anti-Slavery Fair. | MDCCCXLVI.

[20]

12mo. Collation: Half-title, title, imprint, and Contents, pp. [i–vi]; blank, pp. [vii, viii]; text, pp. 1–268. Portrait of William Lloyd Garrison facing title. Size of leaf, untrimmed, 8¼ by 5 inches.

Issued in white boards, printed in gilt, gilt edges, front cover lettered "The | Liberty | Bell. | Twelfth | Massachusetts | Anti-Slavery Fair. | Faneuil Hall." Also issued in printed paper covers, edges untrimmed, with same lettering.

This volume contains "The Falconer. | By J. R. Lowell." Dated at end "Elmwood, Nov. 26, 1845." Pp. 241–244.

1845

The | Missionary Memorial: | A | Literary and Religious Souvenir. | [quotation, 5 lines] | New York: | E. Walker, 114 Fulton Street. | M DCCC XLVI.

12mo. Collation: Half-title, title, copyright (dated 1845) and imprint, Dedication, Preface, and Contents, pp. [i]–xii; text, pp. 1–372; engraved title, separately printed. Size of leaf, trimmed, 7⅞₁₆ by 4⅞₁₆ inches.

Issued in cloth, back lettered "The | Missionary | Memorial | E. Walker N. York." Also issued in stamped morocco.

"The Captive | By James Russell Lowell." fills pp. [47]–51. This volume was reprinted in part, from the same plates, with the title: "The | Evergreen, | a | Christmas, New Year, | and Birthday Gift. | New York: | Leavitt & Allen, 379 Broadway." Lowell's "The Captive" is, as before, on pp. [47]–51.

"Poems | By | Alexander H. Everett," published in Boston by James Munroe & Co., in 1845, contains on p. [9] an extract from the *Boston Miscellany* of October, 1842, being a portion of a review by Lowell of Everett's poem "The Hermitage." It seems scarcely worthy of a place in a set of the first editions of Lowell's writings.

1846

Conversations | on Some of | The Old Poets. | By | James Russell Lowell. | [waved rule] | [quotation, 5 lines] | [waved rule] | Second Edition. | [ornament] | Cambridge: | Published by John Owen. | 1846.

16mo. Collation: Title, copyright (dated 1844) and imprint, Dedication, quotation, and To the Reader,. pp. [i–viii] ; text, pp. [1]–267. Size of leaf, trimmed, 6¾ by 4⁷⁄₁₆ inches.

Issued in cloth, back lettered "Conversations | On Some of | The Old | Poets"; also issued in lithographed paper covers, the date 1846 having been inserted on the first page and without the date 1845, which appears at the bottom of the back on the cover of the first edition.

This second edition was extended from 263 to 267 pages. At the bottom of p. viii there is a new "Note to the Second Edition," dated at end "Sept. 20, 1845." It begins:

"In the second edition a few corrections and verbal alterations have been made, and the First Conversation has been divided into two. In other respects the book remains the same."

Nevertheless there are twelve new lines on p. 9; three new lines on pp. 27, 28; seven new lines on p. 59; and nine new lines on p. 60.

A compilation by H. Hastings Weld, "Scenes in the Lives of the Apostles," Philadelphia, n. d., but copyright 1846, contains, on p. 28, a sonnet headed, "The Way of Life | James Russell Lowell." This is one of the sonnets from "A Year's Life,"

"I saw a gate: a harsh voice spake and said,"

here reprinted with a new title.

1846

The | Ladies' Casket; | containing | a Gem, together with its sentiment, | and a poetical description, for | each day in the week, and | each month in the year. | [rule] | By J. Wesley Hanson. | [rule] | [quotation, 5 lines] | Lowell: | Merrill and Heywood. | Boston: B. B. Mussey. | 1846. |

32mo. Collation: Title, copyright (dated 1846) and imprint, Preface, Dedication, half-title, quotations, pp. [1–8]; text, pp. 9–157; Index, pp. [158]–160. Engraved title, in red, blue, and gold, pasted in, in front. Size of leaf, trimmed, gilt edges, 4½ by 2¾ inches.

Issued in blue cloth, back lettered "The | Ladies' | Casket."

This little volume contains a poem for June, Saturday, on pp. 56–57,

"Sapphire.— { Stately Beauty.",

signed at end "J. R. Lowell." It has never, apparently, been reprinted.

1846

The | American Anti-Slavery | Almanac, | for | 1847. | Being the third year after Bissextile, or Leap Year. | Comprising | The motions of the Sun and Moon, the true places and aspects of the Planets, rising | and setting of the Sun, and the rising, setting, and southing of the Moon.—also, | the Lunations, Conjunctions, Eclipses, Judgments of the Weather, Rising | and Setting of the Planets, Length of Days and Nights, Time of | High Water, &c. &c. | [rule] [quotation, 15 lines] | [rule] | New York: | Published by the American Anti-Slavery Society, 142 Nassau St.; | Boston, 25 Cornhill; Philadelphia, 31 North Fifth St.; | and at the office of the Bugle, Salem, Columbiana Co., Ohio. |

12mo. Collation: Title, p. [1]; text, pp. [2–48]. Size of leaf, trimmed, 7 by 4½ inches.

Issued as a stitched pamphlet, without covers.

This almanac contains the first of the "Biglow Papers," though that title does not appear upon the article. It begins at the top of p. 46: "(From the Boston Courier) | Mister Eddyter:—Our Hosea was down to Bosting last week, and he see | " etc., twenty-nine lines in prose, full measure, signed "Ezekiel Bigelow." Then below, in verse, in double column, seven stanzas, eight lines each, on p. 46, and thirteen stanzas, eight lines each, on p. 47. When this was collected in 1848, in "The Biglow Papers," where it forms No. I, it was headed "A Letter from Mr. Ezekiel Biglow of Jaalam to the Hon. Joseph T. Buckingham, Editor of the Boston Courier, inclosing a Poem of his son, Mr. Hosea Biglow." This heading does not appear in the almanac.

1846

The | Liberty Bell. | Friends of Freedom. | [quotation, 4 lines] | Boston: | National Anti-Slavery Bazaar. | MDCCCXLVII.

12mo. Collation: Half-title, title, imprint, and Contents, pp. [iii]–viii; text, pp. 1–304. Size of leaf, trimmed, 7½ by 4%₁₆ inches.

Issued in cloth, gilt edges, back lettered "The | Liberty | Bell." Also in paper cover, printed in gold, edges untrimmed.

This annual contains: "Extreme Unction. | By James Russell Lowell." Dated at end "Elmwood, Cambridge, U. S." Pp. 240–245.

In "The Pioneer: or Leaves from an Editor's Portfolio.", Lynn, 1846, there is included "The Times, The Manners, and the Men. | By James Russell Lowell." Pp. 172, 173. This is actually an extract from his long poem "A Glance Behind the Curtain.", printed in "Poems," 1844. The text is slightly different, three new lines being substituted for ten lines of the poem as printed in the 1844 volume.

1847

Poems | By | James Russell Lowell. | Second Series. | [rule] | Cambridge: | Published by George Nichols. | Boston: | B. B. Mussey and Company. | 1848.

12mo. Collation: Half-title, title, copyright (dated 1847) and imprint, Dedication, To M. W. L., and Contents, pp. [i–viii];

half-title and text, pp. 1–184. Size of leaf, untrimmed, 7¼ by 4½ inches.

Issued in gray boards, with paper label, "Poems | By | J. R. Lowell | Second Series." A later issue was in cloth, blind-stamped, back lettered in gilt "Lowell's | Poems | Second Series | Ticknor & Co."

Although Mr. Greenslet says that this volume was "published just at the beginning of 1848," it is certain that it was out late in the preceding year. The copy given to Lydia Maria Child has an inscription dated "Dec. 23, 1847," and the inscription in the copy given to Charles F. Briggs is dated "Xmas, 1847." The Briggs copy has one correction in Lowell's autograph. Page 34, line 6, "To the lumberer asleep 'neath thy booming" has the last word corrected to "glooming."

One poem, "The Morning Glory," pp. 131–134, was by Maria Lowell. A foot-note to the "Table of Contents" says, simply, that it "is by another hand."

1847

The | Liberty Bell. | By | Friends of Freedom. | [quotation, 4 lines] | Boston: | National Anti-Slavery Bazaar. | MDCCCXLVIII.

12mo. Collation: Half-title, engraved title (separately printed), title, imprint, and Contents, pp. [i]–viii; text, pp. 1–292. Size of leaf, trimmed, 7 by 4½ inches.

Issued in cloth, back lettered "The | Liberty | Bell".

This annual contains: "An Extract. | By James Russell Lowell." | "Force never yet gained one true victory:". | Dated at end "Elmwood, Cambridge, Massachusetts." Pp. 180–183. This was apparently never collected.

1847

The | Young American's Magazine | of | Self-Improvement. | Combining Literary Entertainment and Instruction with an Effort to | promote the Union of thorough Self-Improvement with every | Department

[25]

of Industry. | Edited by George W. Light. | [quotation, 3 lines] | First Volume. | Boston: Charles H. Peirce, 3 Cornhill, | 1847.

12mo. Collation: Title, copyright (dated 1847) and imprint, advertisement and Postscript, Contents, Prospectus, pp. [1]–10; text, pp. [11]–364. Engraved portrait of Franklin facing title. Size of leaf, trimmed, 7½ by 4⅝ inches. Two advertisements of "Young American Magazine" bound in at end, pp. 1–4, pp. [1]–4.

First issued in six numbers, and then, as described above, in one volume, bound in black cloth.

As no more than this first volume was ever published, it is sought for by collectors and therefore is included here. Lowell contributed three pieces to the magazine:

"Above and Below. | By J. R. Lowell. | Written for the Young American's Magazine." Dated at end "Elmwood, 1846." Pp. 54, 55.

"Hebè. | By J. R. Lowell." Dated at end "Elmwood, 1847." Pp. 143, 144.

"Study for a Head. | By J. R. Lowell." Dated at end "Elmwood, 1847." Pp. 268–270.

1848

Reader! walk up at once (it will soon be too late) and buy | at a perfectly ruinous rate | A | Fable for Critics; | or | Better— | I like, as a thing that the reader's first fancy may strike, | an old fashioned title-page, | such as presents a tabular view of the volume's contents— | A Glance | At a Few of Our Literary Progenies | (Mrs. Malaprop's Word) | From | The Tub of Diogenes; | That is, | a Series of Jokes | By a Wonderful Quiz, | who accompanies himself with a rub-a-dub-dub, full of spirit and grace, | on the top of the tub. | Set forth in | October, the 21st day, in the year '48, | By | G. P. Putnam, Broadway. |

12mo. Collation: Half-title, publisher's list, title (printed in red and black), and copyright (dated 1848), pp. [1–4]; To the Reader, pp. [i]–iii; text, pp. [5]–78. Size of leaf, trimmed at side only, 7⅝ by 5¹⁄₁₆ inches.

Issued in gray boards, with paper label, "A | Fable | for | Critics." Also in stamped cloth, back lettered lengthwise "Fable for Critics."

An examination of the stitching of a loose copy in the original covers shows that in this first edition the half-title and title form one signature, two leaves (without mark); "To the Reader," one signature, two leaves (with signature mark "1"); while the text is six signatures of six leaves each, marked "2", "3", "4", "5", "6" and "7", and one signature of a single leaf, marked "8".

The head-line throughout, which reads, "A Fable for the Critics," is printed in large capitals and there is a rule below the head-line on every page.

Considered bibliographically, the "Fable for Critics" is one of the most interesting of Lowell's books. "About 600 lines" had been written in the fall of 1847, which were copied off and sent in December as a New Year's gift to Charles F. Briggs, to whom he presented the profits from the sale of the book. Briggs acknowledged the manuscript in a letter written the latter part of January, 1848. He said, in part:

"I accepted your most noble present with as much freedom from anything bearing a resemblance of pride as the spirit in which you offered it, as I should have done had it been money instead of money's worth. Happily by the use of my pen I earn my bread in sufficient abundance, and therefore I do not need your kind gift, but it will give me great pleasure to receive it, whatever it may produce; the use which I at once resolved to make of it I will explain to you by and by.

"I think as you do that it will be marvelously popular and salable, and I shall grace it with some sketches if I can get them done to suit me. I think it will sell much better by being published in New York than in Boston."

And a few days later he again writes: "I will try to get to press at once and when I send you the first proofs you must send me back some more copy, but don't let it interfere with your review articles nor with anything else that will produce you cash or comforts of any kind. When I received the poem I determined to appropriate the profits of it in this manner: one third should be invested for Queen Mab, to be given her on her eighteenth birthday; one third to be disposed of in the same manner for my little angel; and the other third to be given to Page, for which he should paint your portrait for me and mine for you. This would be making the best disposition of the fund that I could devise, and I think will not be displeasing to you. If the profits should be small, I will divide them equally between the little ones."

On March 26, Lowell wrote to Briggs that he was "waiting for pleasanter weather in order to finish" the poem. He adds: "I ought not to have sent you any part of it till I had finished entirely."

The following extracts are from letters of Charles F. Briggs heretofore unpublished:

April 22. "I cannot make any definite arrangements about publishing the 'Fable' until I know the size of it. I want Putnam should publish it because he is not only the most liberal and intelligent of the tribe of publishers, but his London house will afford him better facilities for giving it a circulation there than any other publisher has."

June 3. "Putnam will Publish the Fable as soon as the remainder of it comes to hand, and in very handsome style."

September 16. "I send you another form of the fable, and have left it for you to correct. We have been delayed waiting for paper."

October 3. "I send you the revises as far as they go, they have now commenced printing the first form and will soon make a finish of it, so, if you intend adding a preface, it will be well to have it here soon. I don't wish to hurry you, and feel too much mortified at the trouble you have already been at, on my account, to ask you to add anything more; but Putnam having advertised the work for September he will be in a hurry to get it out."

October 6. "I had the title-page already set up precisely as you suggested, but I happily conceived the idea of printing it in two colors, after the manner of Pickering's new old books, and as Putnam is taken with the idea it will be done. I will send you a proof on Monday."

The published letters of Lowell to Briggs show that the last of the copy was sent on August 22. On October 4: "I send half the proof to-day—t' other to-morrow," and in the same letter: "I wish to see title-page and preface." Two days later he wrote:

"Print the title-page thus:—

"'Reader, walk up' etc. as far as 'ruinous rate' in large italics in old fashioned style in an inverted cone

A

down to   Fable for Critics   in very large caps. Then the rest in small caps properly broken up so as to conceal the fact of the rhyme."

Although the rhymed title-page says, "Set forth in October, the 21st day," the book was not published until the 25th. On that day Briggs wrote to Lowell:

"I believe that there is no error in the Fable, typographically, but the title is most wretchedly printed, and by an accident the advertisement of

Putnam which should have been placed on a fly leaf at the end of the volume was so printed as to face the title, and it was not discovered until the book was bound, and Putnam on board the steamer. By a strange succession of accidents it was delayed a fortnight and at last botched. But, as only 1000 copies have been printed, it shall be corrected in the next edition, which I have little doubt will soon be called for. The literati have been itching for it the past month, and all who have had a glimpse of it are charmed with it. Putnam's leaving for London was a sudden move which disarranged matters so that the printing of the title page was given to the wrong person, and as he was anxious to take some copies with him he ordered the binder to send for it so that it was not seen, and I could not obtain a revise myself. Then it so happened that the order given for the paper was not for sufficient quantity so that they had to wait near a week to get more from the mill. They advertised it Saturday [October 21st], but the copies were not obtained until this morning. They are mortified about it, but nobody was to blame, as they say when a steamboat blows up. I felt very much vexed about the matter on your account for I meant that book should be elegantly got up. However, it has beauty enough, and goodness enough, to overcome much more serious blunders."

On October 6, Lowell had written: "I wish you would do up a copy with 'author's and so forths,' *dated New York,* and put it into Ticknor's first box directed to Dr. O. W. Holmes, Boston, and also one directed to Professor Felton, Cambridge, in Ticknor's or Nichols's as it may chance." And in the letter of October 25 from which the preceding extract is quoted Briggs wrote: "I will have the copies of the 'Fable' directed and sent as you desire, and if you wish more copies will send them. But you had better wait for the second edition before you send any to your very particular friends for I fear that they will laugh at our New York publishers, for the style in which the book is issued."

After the book was out, on November 12, Briggs wrote to Lowell, telling of published criticisms, that "Page repeats it all by heart off hand," and then says:

"The little errors of typography and bungling manner in which the title page was struck off annoyed me a good deal, for I knew what a nice eye you possess. But the next edition shall be better, you may be sure. Craighead is a very good printer; he was too busy to do the Fable, and Putnam gave it to a new, but a reputed good printer, by way of trying him. If our prin ers, in New York, are not quite so nice as yours in Cambridge it is probably because they have so much business on their hands. But that is not a valid excuse for them, I know."

In a later letter, dated simply "Saturday, Nov. 1848," but evidently November 27, he writes:

"Every copy of the Fable was sold a fort-night ago, and the second edition is now about two-thirds stereotyped. I have read it very carefully. If you have the preface ready be so good as to send it immediately."

This second edition was, apparently, not ready on December 20, when Lowell wrote to Sydney Howard Gay:

"Briggs must give you a copy of the second edition, in which the atrocious misprints of the other will be corrected, and to which I have prefixed a new preface."

The misprints of the first edition were, aside from the title-page, not so "atrocious" as the above statement would lead us to expect. The following errors were corrected by Lowell in his autograph in the copy of the book given by him to Thomas Wentworth Higginson and which was acquired by Mr. Chamberlain:

P. 6, l. 8: "woo'd" changed to "wood"
P. 16, l. 2: "in shade" changed to "in the shade"
P. 35, l. 13: "on the ocean" changed to "with the ocean"
P. 42, l. 13: "You're" changed to "Your"
P. 43, l. 25: "cords" changed to "chords"
P. 50, l. 13: "pieces" changed to "princes"
P. 54, l. 12: "the hunting" changed to "in hunting"
P. 65, l. 22: "that" changed to "those"
P. 68, l. 4: "And if" changed to "As if"
P. 68, l. 5: "As if" changed to "And as if"
P. 70, l. 19: "corn, or" changed to "corn is, or"
P. 74, l. 2: "smile to a frown" changed to "frown to a smile"

On February 7, 1849, Briggs wrote: "The Fable has gone to a third edition of 1000, at least I see it is so advertised." On March 15, 1849, Briggs tells Lowell:

"Putnam offered me half profits on the sale of the Fable, but I agreed with him for ten percent on the amount of sales at the retail price. I have had no settlement with him yet, nor have I received anything from him."

And again on September 17, 1849:

"The Fable has sold well, but exactly how well I do not know. I have not yet received a copper on account of it, but I shall get something before long and will remember you on account."

And again on November 28, 1849:

"Don't misunderstand my allusions to the Fable. I supposed that you would like to know how it had sold. Something less than 3,000 copies have been disposed of, and I believe that another edition will be got out before long."

In the collected edition of the "Poetical Works," Boston, 1857, the date in the imprint was altered to "October, the 31st day." Mr. Scudder inadvertently gives this as the date of "the first title-page" and Mr. Greenslet copies his error.

An author is seldom an authoritative source of bibliographical information about his books, and recollections of forty years earlier can hardly be expected to agree exactly with the facts as narrated in letters written at the time. And it was so with Lowell. To the edition of the "Fable for Critics" published in October, 1890, he prefixes this note:

"This *jeu d'esprit* was extemporized, I may fairly say, so rapidly was it written, purely for my own amusement and with no thought of publication. I sent daily instalments of it to a friend in New York, the late Charles F. Briggs. He urged me to let it be printed, and I at last consented to its anonymous publication. The secret was kept till several persons had laid claim to its authorship."

The letters show that about "six hundred lines" were written sometime before November 13, 1847, and on that day he copied out "Emerson" as a specimen. This portion was "all written with one impulse and was the work of not a great many hours." It was copied off and sent to Briggs on December 31, 1847. On February 1, 1848, he had in addition, "and exclusive of Emerson, etc., about a hundred lines," written "chiefly about Willis and Longfellow." On March 26 no further progress had been made and he was telling Briggs: "I hope you will write and give me a spur." On May 12 he had "begun upon the 'Fable' again fairly," and was "making some headway." On May 19 he wrote to Gay: "Tell Briggs I have finished John Neal, Hawthorne, Cooper, *myself,* and something more, and that there will not be more than twelve hundred lines." On August 22 he sent the last of the manuscript. Meanwhile Briggs had more than once been asking him for copy.

1848

Reader! walk up at once (it will soon be too late) and | buy at a perfectly ruinous rate | A | Fable For Critics; | or, better, | (I like, as a thing that the reader's first fancy may strike, | an old-fashioned title-page, | such as presents a tabular view of the volume's contents) | A Glance | At a Few of our Literary Progenies | (Mrs. Malaprop's word) | From | The Tub of Diogenes; | A Vocal and Musical Medley. | That is, | A Series of Jokes | By a Wonderful Quiz, | who accompanies himself with a rub-a-dub-dub, full of spirit and grace, | on the top of the tub. | Set forth in | October, the 21st day, in the year '48: | G. P. Putnam, Broadway.

12mo. Collation: Title (printed in red and black), copyright (dated 1848) and imprint, pp. [i, ii]; To the Reader, pp. [iii]–v; blank, p. [vi]; A Preliminary Note to the Second Edition, 6 pp.; text, pp. [7]–80; publisher's advertisements, pp. 9–16. Size of leaf, trimmed, 7½ by 4⅞ inches.

Issued in boards with paper label, and also in stamped cloth, back lettered "Fable | for | Critics."

There were several editions printed from the stereotype plates which were made after the 1000 copies of the first edition printed from type were disposed of. The "Preliminary Note to the Second Edition" was at first separately printed and pasted down on the fourth leaf of the first signature. It was not inserted at all in the earlier copies. A study of several copies in the original bindings shows a different "make-up" in the printing. The earliest printing consists of three signatures of twelve leaves each, the last ending on page 72. The next two leaves, pp. 73–76, form a fourth signature, and the last two leaves, pp. 77–80, form a fifth. The only signature marks are "1" on p. [iii] and 2* on p. 33, but the stitching is very evident in the copy examined. This copy does not contain, and apparently never has contained, the three extra leaves, the "Preliminary Note."

The second printing has also three signatures of twelve leaves each, the last ending with p. 72. Then comes a signature of eight leaves, being pp. 73–80 of text and eight pages of advertisements not in the earlier copies. These pages are 9–16 of Putnam's Catalogue. The three leaves of the "Preliminary Note" were, in most copies, pasted in before the book was bound, but Mr. Chamberlain owned a copy in which the three leaves had evidently been inserted after the book was bound.

In a third form the title leaf is a separate signature, followed by three signatures of twelve leaves each, the last ending on page 68, the "Preliminary Note," three leaves, being included in the first signature. Pp. 69–80 form a fourth signature, six leaves. The copy of this form which I have examined has the last line of the imprint, "G. P. Putnam, 10 Park Place." The title was not reset, but merely a change made in the stereotype plate.

The only signature marks in any of these stereotype editions are "1" on page [iii] and 2* on page 33.

Some of the more important typographical differences between the first and later editions are:

No half-title in the second edition. The first edition has a half-title.

Extra line, "A Vocal and Musical Medley," is inserted in its proper place on the title-page. This line was omitted in the first edition.

A printer's imprint on verso of title, below the copyright. There is no imprint in the first edition.

No waved rule above "To the Reader." In the first edition there is a waved rule.

Text is numbered [5] to 78 in the first edition; [7] to 80 in the second.

No rule below the head-lines. In the first edition there is a straight rule below the head-line at the top of each page of text.

1848

Water Celebration, | Boston, October 25, 1848. | Exercises at the Fountain.

Folio. A single leaf, printed on one side only. The above is the heading, followed by Order of Exercises, the third number being "III. Ode. | By James Russell Lowell, Esq., | To be sung by the School Children." Then follows the poem, eight stanzas of six lines each.

This programme was printed before the celebration and therefore ante-dates the pamphlet usually considered as the first edition of Lowell's "Ode." This account of the celebration has the title: "Celebration | of the | Introduction | Of the | Water of Cochituate Lake | into the | City of Boston. | [waved rule] | October 25, 1848. | [waved rule] | [Seal of Boston] | [waved rule] | Boston: | J. H. Eastburn, City Printer." The "Ode. | By James Russell Lowell, Esq. | Sung by the School Children." is on pp. 21, 22.

1848

Melibœus-Hipponax. | [rule] | The | Biglow Papers, | Edited, | With an Introduction, Notes, Glossary, | and Copious Index, | By | Homer Wilbur, A.M., | Pastor of the First Church in Jaalam, and (Prospective) Member of | many Literary, Learned and Scientific Societies, | (for which see page v.) | [quotation, 5 lines] | Cambridge: | Published by George Nichols. | 1848.

12mo. Collation: Notices of an Independent Press, pp. [1]–12; half-title, title, copyright (dated 1848) and imprint, Note to the Title-Page, Introduction, and Contents, pp. [i]–xxxii; text, Glossary, and Index, pp. 1–163. Size of leaf, untrimmed, 7⅛ by 4⁹⁄₁₆ inches.

Issued in glazed boards, untrimmed, with paper label. Also in stamped cloth, back lettered "Biglow | Papers".

I have seen a single copy in plain pale green paper covers, un-printed, edges trimmed, size 6⅞ by 4⅜ inches. This last was probably an advance issue sent out for review.

Mr. Cooke states that some copies were issued without the preliminary leaves, "Notices of an Independent Press," but this is undoubtedly an error, as the half-title and title are leaves 7 and 8 of the first signature "a", followed by signature "b", eight leaves, and "c", six leaves. The text itself begins with a new series of signatures, the mark "1" being on p. [1].

Copies for the New York market—perhaps they may be called a second issue—have five-line imprint: "Cambridge: | Published by George Nichols. | New York: | George P. Putnam, 155 Broadway. | 1848." This New York issue seems to have been bound at the same time, as the stamp is identical.

On June 16, 1846, Lowell wrote to the editor of the *Anti-Slavery Standard:* "You will find a squib of mine in this week's Courier. I wish it to continue anonymous, for I wish slavery to think it has as many enemies as possible." This was the first of these Biglow Papers, "A Letter from Mr. Ezekiel Biglow," which appeared in the *Boston Courier* of June 17, 1846, and which was reprinted in the "Anti-Slavery Almanac" for 1848, as already noted. Of the other eight pieces which make up the volume, four appeared in the *Boston Courier* and the other four in the *Anti-Slavery Standard,* the last being in the *Standard* of September 28, 1848.

On September 2, 1848, he had "got between twenty and thirty pages already printed," and he added: "It is the hardest book to print that ever I had anything to do with." "It made fifty pages more than" he expected, but on November 10 he wrote: "It will be out, I suppose, today. The first edition, of 1500 copies, "were all gone in a week—so that the book was actually out of print before a second edition could be struck off from the plates."

Charles F. Briggs made the arrangements with Putnam for the New York edition. In a letter dated simply "New York, Saturday Oct. 1848", he wrote to Lowell:

"Putnam says that you may put his name into 100 copies for his London agency and 500 for New York, if you would like for him to attend to the sale and distribution here."

I have not seen a copy with the London imprint.

1848

The Vision | of | Sir Launfal. | By | James Russell Lowell. | [rule] | Cambridge: | Published by George Nichols. | 1848.

12mo. Collation: Half-title, title, copyright (dated 1848) and imprint, Note, pp. [i–v]; half-title and text, pp. [1]–27. Size of leaf, untrimmed, 7¼ by 4⅜ inches.

Issued in yellow glazed boards, front cover lettered "The Vision | of | Sir Launfal." within a border. Also in pale brown boards, edges untrimmed, with paper label, "The Vision of | Sir Launfal."

On February 1, 1848, Lowell wrote to Briggs, referring to this poem: "I shall probably publish it by itself next summer." It was, however, published on December 18. On the 22d of that month he wrote to Briggs: "I shall send you Sir Launfal in a day or two. I could not get copies enough yesterday." On the 31st Briggs replied: "Sir Launfal arrived at a very bad time, when all the booksellers had made their arrangements for their holiday sales, and Putnam had got all his advertisements and had his hands too full to attend to anything more. I do not think there is any danger of its being damned with faint praise, for its merits are of a kind that can be appreciated by the superficial as well as the thoughtful readers."

The "Anti-Slavery Harp," Boston, 1848, contains on pp. 45, 46, "Are ye Truly Free?" This, as noted, had already appeared in "The Liberty Minstrel," 1844, and "Poems," 1844.

1848

The | Liberty Bell. | By | Friends of Freedom. | [quotation, 4 lines] | Boston: | National Anti-Slavery Bazaar. | MDCCCXLIX

12mo. Collation: Half-title, title, imprint, and Contents, pp. [i]–viii; text, pp. 1–292, portrait frontispiece and engraved title. Size of leaf, trimmed, 7 by 4½ inches.

Issued in cloth, gilt edges, back lettered "The | Liberty | Bell".

This annual contains: "The Burial of Theobald. | By James Russell Lowell." Pp. 269–274.

It seems never to have been collected.

1848

The | Gallery of Mezzotints: | An Annual | for | 1849. | With twenty-one superb engravings. | New York: | M. H. Newman & Company, | 199 Broadway. | MDCCCXLIX.

8vo. Collation: Title, imprint, Contents, and Embellishments, pp. [1–7]; blank, p. [8]; text, pp. [9]–224. Twenty-one mezzotints, separately printed, inserted as per list on p. [7]. Size of leaf, trimmed, 8¼ by 5¾ inches.

Issued in stamped morocco, gilt edges, back lettered "Gallery of Mezzotints | 1849."

This volume contains "To Lamartine. | By James Russell Lowell." Pp. 9–13. A foot-note in the Table of Contents says: "From the National A. S. Standard."

This poem appeared first in the *Anti-Slavery Standard* for August 3, 1848, and next in the present volume, published late in 1848. It was collected in the second volume of "Poems," 1849.

1849

Poems | by | James Russell Lowell. | In two Volumes. | Vol. I. [Vol. II.] | Boston: | Ticknor, Reed, and Fields. | M DCCC XLIX.

2 vols., 12mo. Collation: Vol. I: Half-title, title, copyright (dated 1849) and imprint, Dedication, Note, and Contents, pp. [i–xii]; half-title and text, pp. 1–251. Publishers' list dated "December, 1849." bound in, in front, pp. 1–4. Vol. II: Half-title, title, copyright and imprint, and Contents, pp. [i]–vii; half-title and text, pp. 1–254. Size of leaf, half-trimmed, 7⅛ by 4½ inches.

Issued in gray boards with paper label, "Lowell's | Poems. | In Two Volumes. | Vol. I. [Vol. II.]" Also in brown cloth, back lettered "Lowell's | Poems | Vol. I. [Vol. II.] | Ticknor & Co.", and, as a holiday edition, perhaps, in red cloth, full gilt sides, and gilt edges.

These two volumes were printed from the same stereotype plates as the "Poems," 1844, and "Poems, Second Series," 1848, but with alterations. The following are the principal points of difference:

Vol. I

The half-title, title, and copyright were reset. The original copyright was taken out by John Owen, and was dated 1843. In this volume the date was changed to 1849 and James Russell Lowell's name appears instead of Owen's.

The Dedication, pp. [v]–vii, is identical. P. [viii], blank in the 1844 volume, here has this note: "This edition is a revised one, but as the volumes which form the substance of it had been stereotyped, it was found easier to cancel than to correct. Accordingly, several poems and parts of poems have been left out of the first volume, and their places supplied in most instances by selections from an earlier volume published in 1841. These intercalated pieces will be found sufficiently designated by the dates appended to each. The second volume has been made correspondent in size with its fellow, by the addition of some poems more lately written."

"A Legend of Brittany," which filled pp. 3–63 of the 1844 volume, here occupies only pp. 3–44, stanzas xii, xv, xx, xxi, xxiii, xxiv, xxxvii, xxxix to xlv, xlviii, xlix, liii, and liv of Part I, vi to xi, xvi, xxi, xxv, xxvii, xxxii, xxxiii, li, lii, lix, lx, lxiii, and lxiv of Part II, being omitted, and the stanzas renumbered. Then comes the half-title, here pp. [45, 46], and, to fill up pp. 47–66, the following poems have been inserted from "A Year's Life":

"Threnodia." Dated "1839" at end.

"The Sirens." Dated "Nantasket, July, 1840" at end.

"Serenade." Dated "1840" at end.

"Irenè." Dated "1840" at end.

The two books then correspond as far as p. 101. "The Dirge," which filled pp. 101–105 of the 1844 volume, was omitted, the space being filled by:

"With a Pressed Flower." Dated "1840."

"The Beggar." Dated "1839."

Both of these had been included in "A Year's Life." The last fifty lines of "Rhœcus" were omitted, as also the next two pieces, "Song." and "In Sadness." In this space, pp. 126–133, were inserted:

"The Falcon." Not dated.

"My Love." Dated "1840."

"Trial." Not dated.

The first of these was taken from "Poems, Second Series," 1848; the second had appeared in "A Year's Life," 1841, and the third appears here for the first time in book-form.

From p. 134 to p. 141, the two correspond. After this no effort seems to have been made to retain the pagination of the old plates. Two poems, "Forgetfulness" and "A Reverie," filling pp. 142–147, were cut out, but instead of trying to fill in new matter, the pagination of the next poem, "Love," was altered, and so on to the end. "Fantasy," pp. 195–197, was omitted, and "To the Memory of Hood" inserted in its place. "Silence," pp. 213–215, was omitted, and "Thistle-downs," filling only one page, was inserted. Both of these are here first collected. More than half of "A Chippewa Legend"—from the middle of p. 222 to the end, p. 227—was omitted. In the 1844 volume there were thirty-seven sonnets, but thirteen of these—numbers III, IV, V, XI, XII, XVI, XVIII, XIX, XX, XXIX, XXXIV, XXXV, and XXXVI—were omitted in 1849. Three new ones,

"I would not have this perfect love of ours,"

"For this true nobleness I seek in vain,"

"I thought our love at full, but I did err,"

were inserted. The first and second of these were taken from "A Year's Life"; the third was from "Poems, Second Series."

The 1844 volume contains 279 pages of text, while this 1849 volume has only 251.

FIRST EDITIONS OF LOWELL

Vol. II

In the same way the text of the 1848 volume, "Poems, Second Series," is identical with Vol. II of this 1849 edition as far as p. 149. "Anti-Texas," filling pp. 150–156, was cut out, and "The Falconer," filling pp. 157–159, slightly altered, was transferred to Vol. I, with the title "The Falcon." In the place of these two pieces were inserted three others, here first collected:
"Eurydice."
"She Came and Went."
"To W. L. Garrison."
The 1848 volume ended with p. 184. Pp. 185–254 of the 1849 volume contain the following pieces:
"The Vision of Sir Launfal."
"Ode to France."
"Kossuth."
"To Lamartine."
"A Parable."
"Ode Written for the Celebration of the Introduction of the Cochituate Water into the City of Boston."
"Lines Suggested by the Graves of Two English Soldiers on Concord Battle Ground."
"To ——."
"Freedom."
"Bibliolatres."
"Beaver Brook."
"To John G. Palfrey."
Several of these pieces had already been printed in the *Anti-Slavery Standard*, but they are here first collected.
The Table of Contents in each volume was probably entirely reset.
From these same stereotype plates editions of the "Poems" were from time to time printed, the "Seventh Edition"—perhaps the last—being dated 1857.
On November 25, 1849, Lowell wrote to Charles F. Briggs:
"My new edition will be out about the 10th of December, and I think that with Ticknor publishing I shall, for the first time, make something by my poems. I shall clear at least $100 by the first edition, and every subsequent one will be clear gain, as I shall have no expense about the plates."
Three days later Briggs replied: "I am anxiously waiting for the two volumes," but there seems to have been a further delay in the publication of the books. On January 28, 1850, he wrote: "Thank you for your two precious volumes; they certainly ought to satisfy you when they so more than satisfy your friends."

"The Canzonet," Montpelier, 1849, contains three poems by Lowell: "Lines on the Death of Charles T. Torrey," "The Contrast," and "The Outcast." All of these had been printed in earlier books. "The Outcast" is merely an extract from the poem "The Forlorn," with a new title.

1849

The Works | of the late | Edgar Allan Poe: | With | Notices of his Life and Genius. | By | N. P. Willis, J. R. Lowell, and R. W. Griswold. | In two volumes. | [rule] | Vol. I. | Tales. | [rule] | New York: | J. S. Redfield, Clinton Hall. | 1850.

12mo. Collation: Title, copyright (dated 1849), To the Reader, and Contents, pp. [i–vi]; "Edgar A. Poe. | By James Russell Lowell.", pp. vii–xiii; "Death of E. A. Poe. By N. P. Willis," pp. xiv–xx; text, pp. 1–483. Publisher's list bound in at end, pp. 1–4. Frontispiece portrait of Poe. Size of leaf, untrimmed, 7⅜ by 4⅝ inches.

Issued in cloth, back lettered "Works | of | Edgar A. Poe | Vol. 1. | Tales."

This first volume of Poe's works, edited by R. W. Griswold, contains Lowell's article (pp. vii–xiii), which had appeared in *Graham's Magazine* for February, 1845, as No. XVII of the series "Our Contributors." It is not included in the collected editions of Lowell's works, though Stoddard and Woodberry included it in their editions of Poe's works.

This edition of Poe's works was in four volumes: Vols. I and II published late in 1849 (though the titles are dated 1850), Vol. III in 1850, and Vol. IV in 1856. The other volumes contain nothing by Lowell.

"Gems from the Spirit Mine," London, 1850, contains, on p. 70, "The Fatherland" by James Russell Lowell. This poem had, however, already appeared in the "Poems" of 1844.

1850

Memory and Hope. | Boston: | Ticknor, Reed, and Fields. | M DCCC LI. |

8vo. Collation: Half-title, title, copyright (dated 1850) and imprint, Dedication, Poem, and Contents, pp. [i]–xii; text, pp. 1–244. Size of leaf, trimmed, 8⅛ by 5⅜ inches.

Issued in cloth, gilt edges, back lettered "Memory | and |

Hope." Also in stamped morocco, gilt gauffred edges, and perhaps in other bindings.

This volume contains: "The First Snow-fall." Signed at end "J. R.
Lowell." Pp. 19–21.
This poem had appeared first in the *Anti-Slavery Standard* for Decem-
ber 27, 1849. As collected in "Under the Willows," 1868, it was revised.

1850

The | Liberty Bell. | By | Friends of Freedom. | [quota-
tion, 4 lines] | Boston: | National Anti-Slavery Ba-
zaar. | MDCCCLI.

12mo. Collation: Half-title, engraved title (separately printed),
title, imprint, and Contents, pp. [i]–viii; text, pp. 1–304. Size of
leaf, trimmed, 7⅜ by 4⅝ inches.
Issued in cloth, gilt edges, back lettered "The | Liberty |
Bell."

This issue of "The Liberty Bell" contains the first appearance of
"Yussouf. | By James Russell Lowell.", dated at end "Elmwood, Cam-
bridge, U. S." Pp. 303, 304. It was collected in "Under the Willows,"
1868.

"The Boston Book," Boston, 1850, contains "The Syrens" by Lowell,
filling pp. 30–33. This poem had already appeared in "A Year's Life,"
1841.

1852

Garden Walks With the Poets. | By Mrs. C. M. Kirk-
land. | New-York: | G. P. Putnam & Company, 10
Park Place. | 1852.

12mo. Collation: Title, copyright (dated 1852), Preface, List of
Poems, List of Authors, pp. [i]–xii; text, pp. [9]–340. Engraved
title. Size of leaf, trimmed, 7⁵⁄₁₆ by 5⅛ inches.
Issued in stamped cloth, back lettered "Garden | Walks | with |
the | Poets | Mrs. Kirkland | New York | Putnam & Co."

Besides "The Dandelion," which fills pp. 52–54, and which had appeared before in "Poems, Second Series," 1848, as "To the Dandelion," this volume contains two pieces by Lowell:

"A Day in June. | J. R. Lowell." Pp. 126–128.

"Winter Piece. | James Russell Lowell." Pp. 291, 292.

The first of these was collected in "Under the Willows," 1868, but with the title altered to "Al Fresco." The second was never collected.

In "Selections from the Writings and Speeches of William Lloyd Garrison.", 1852, is included, as part of the prefatory matter, Lowell's poem "The Day of Small Things." This appeared under this title in the *Anti-Slavery Standard* for October 16, 1848, and was collected in the second volume of "Poems," 1849, but with the title "To W. L. Garrison," under which title it is found in later editions of the author's works.

1853

Thalatta: | A | Book for the Sea-side. | [quotation, 4 lines] | Boston: | Ticknor, Reed, and Fields. | M DCCC LIII.

12mo. Collation: Title, copyright (dated 1853) and imprint, quotations, and Contents, pp. [i]–viii; text, pp. 1–206. Publishers' list, dated "April, 1853", bound in, in front, pp. 1–8. Size of leaf, half-trimmed, 7⅛ by 5⅝ inches.

Issued in cloth, back lettered "Thalatta | A Book | for | the Sea-side | Ticknor & Co."

This volume contains "Appledore." Signed at end, "J. R. Lowell." Pp. 61–63. This had appeared in *Graham's Magazine* for February, 1851. It was intended to be a part of the volume to be called "The Nooning," which Lowell was for many years planning to bring out. In sending a copy of the two-volume "Poems," 1849, to Charles F. Briggs, Lowell wrote: "My next volume, I think, will show an advance. It is to be called 'The Nooning.'" In June, 1853, he wrote to the same correspondent: "I have the 'Nooning' to finish—which *shall* turn out well." The plan was never carried out, though most of the material intended for the volume was included in "Under the Willows," published in 1868. In December of that year Lowell wrote: "And the 'Nooning.' Sure enough, where is it? The 'June Idyl' (written in '51 or '52) is a part of what I had written as the induction to it. The description of spring in one of the 'Biglow Papers' is another fragment of the same, tagged with rhyme for the nonce. So is a passage in 'Mason and Slidell,' beginning 'Oh, strange new world.' The 'Voyage to Vinland,' the 'Pictures from Appledore,' and 'Fitz-Adam's Story' were written for the 'Nooning,' as originally planned. So, you see, I had made some progress."

1854

The | Poetical Works | of | John Keats. | With a Life. | [rule] | Boston: | Little, Brown and Company. | New York: Evans and Dickerson. | Philadelphia: Lippincott, Grambo and Co. | M. DCCC. LIV.

16mo. Collation: Title, copyright (dated 1854) and imprint, Contents, and Life, pp. [i]–xxxvi; half-title and text, pp. [1]–415. Portrait of Keats facing title. Size of leaf, trimmed, 6¾ by 4¼ inches. Publishers' list bound in, in front, pp. 1–4.

Issued in cloth with paper label, "The | British Poets. | Poems of | Keats. 1855."

Lowell wrote the prefatory Life, "The Life of Keats." Signed at end "J. R. L." Pp. [vii]–xxxvi. This was collected later, though partly rewritten, in the second series of "Among My Books."

On April 20, 1854, Lowell wrote to the printer Mr. Bolles:

"You can begin printing from any editions of Keats's poems—putting the 'Endymion' first as it now stands. There is nothing to be done to it in the way of editing. Before you get through that, I will have the other poems (of Keats) arranged & prefix a sketch of his life."

1854

The | Poetical Works | of | William Wordsworth, | D.C.L., Poet Laureate, etc., etc. | Vol. I. [Vol. II. to Vol. VII.] | [rule] | Boston: | Little, Brown, and Company. | New York: Evans and Dickerson. | Philadelphia: Lippincott, Grambo, and Co. | M. DCCC. LIV.

7 vols., 16mo. Collation, Vol. I: Title, copyright (dated 1854) and imprint, Poem, Contents, pp. [i]–vii; "Sketch of Wordsworth's Life.", pp. [ix]–xl; text, pp. 1–381; Notes, pp. [382]–384. Portrait facing title. Publishers' lists bound in, in front, pp. 1–4. Vol. II: Title, copyright and imprint, and Contents, pp.

[i]–x; text and Notes, pp. 1–406; Vol. III: Title, copyright and imprint, and Contents, pp. [i]–x; text and Notes, pp. 1–342; Vol. IV: Title, copyright and imprint, and Contents, pp. [i]–xii; text and Notes, pp. 1–367. Vol. V: Title, copyright and imprint, and Contents, pp. [i]–vi; text, Notes, Appendix, and Indexes, pp. 1–366. Vol. VI: Title, copyright and imprint, and Contents, pp. [i–iii]; text and Notes, pp. 1–371. Vol. VII: Title, copyright and imprint, and Contents, pp. [i–iii]; text, Notes, and Appendix, pp. 1–414. Size of leaf, trimmed, 6¾ by 4¼ inches.

Issued in cloth, back lettered "The | British | Poets | Wordsworth | I."

To this edition of Wordsworth's works in seven volumes, Lowell contributed the "Sketch of Wordsworth's Life.", pp. [ix]–xl. It was collected in "Among my Books," second series, 1876, but largely rewritten.

The first, third, and fourth stanzas of "Stanzas of Freedom," which were printed in "Poems," 1844, appear under the title of "Hymn" in James Freeman Clarke's pamphlet "The Rendition of Anthony Burns," Boston, 1854. This pamphlet is therefore not a first edition of Lowell.

1854

The | Knickerbocker Gallery: | A Testimonial | To the Editor of the | Knickerbocker Magazine | From its Contributors. | With forty-eight Portraits on Steel, from Original Pictures | engraved expressly for this work. | New York: | Samuel Hueston, 348 Broadway. | [small rule] | MDCCCLV.

8vo. Collation: Title, copyright (dated 1854) and imprint, Contents, List of Engravings, and Preface, pp. [vii]–xiv; text, pp. [15]–505. Frontispiece, engraved title, and plates facing pp. 15, 23, 27, 39, 59, 63, 81, 83, 97, 113, 131, 135, 145, 147, 161, 163, 187, 189, 209, 211, 219, 235, 247, 249, 269, 277, 323, 329, 345, 347, 373, 375, 383, 393, 397, 421, 433, 437, 449, 451, 453, 457, 465, 467, 479, 481, 493, 503. Size of leaf, trimmed, 8¾ by 6 inches.

Issued in stamped cloth, back lettered "The | Knickerbocker | Gallery." Also issued in morocco binding.

To this volume Lowell contributed "Masaccio | Brancacci Chapel, Florence. | By James Russell Lowell." Pp. 381, 382. It was collected in "Under the Willows," 1868.

1855

The | Poetical Works | of | Dr. John Donne, | With a Memoir. | [rule] | Boston: | Little, Brown and Company. | Shepard, Clark and Co. | New York: James S. Dickerson. | Philadelphia: J. B. Lippincott and Co. | M. DCCC. LV.

16mo. Collation: Title, imprint, Dedication (signed "John Donne"), pp. [1]–4; Contents, pp. [v]–x; "Some account | of the | Life of Dr. John Donne.", pp. [xi]–xxii; text, pp. 1–431. Publishers' lists bound in, in front, pp. 1–8. Size of leaf, trimmed, 6¾ by 4¼ inches.

Issued in cloth, back lettered "The | British Poets | Donne".

Lowell edited this edition of Donne's poems. He did not write the Life, as this note appears at the bottom of p. xi: "This is an abridgement of Walton's Life, and is taken from the edition of Donne's Poems published in 1719."

That he prepared copy for the work and read the proof is shown by the following letter addressed to his printer, Mr. Bolles:

"I have queried 'Vol. I.' in the Donne proofs. The edition we print from has exactly 300 pages of 35 lines each. You can reckon from this. I should think he would make one plump volume, and readers don't like your lean & hungry ones any more than Caesar did. . . .

"I can give you copy for Donne as fast as you like.

"Will you also ask Mr. Brown the next time you see him if he has an old edition of Donne? Either of 1633 or 35? If not will he send me the first Vol. of the last edit. of D's Works published at London in 1839 by Alford, if it contains a life?"

It was a copy of this edition the margins of which Lowell filled with emendations, then mislaid, and which was afterwards found and published by the Grolier Club of New York.

1855

The | Poetical Works | of | Percy Bysshe Shelley, | Edited | By Mrs. Shelley. | With a Memoir. | [quotation, 3 lines] | In three volumes. | Volume I. [Volume II.] [Volume III.] | [rule] | Boston: | Little, Brown, and Company. | New York: James S. Dickerson. | Philadelphia: Lippincott, Grambo and Co. | M. DCCC. LV.

3 vols., 16mo. Collation, Vol. I: Title, copyright (dated 1855) and imprint, Dedication, Contents, Preface, Postscript, and Memoir, pp. [i]–xli; half-title and text, pp. [1]–449. Portrait facing title. Publishers' list bound in, in front, pp. 1–8. Vol. II: Title, copyright and imprint, and Contents, pp. [i]–vi; half-title and text, pp. [1]–499. Vol. III: Title, copyright and imprint, pp. [i]–vi; half-title and text, pp. [1]–450. Size of leaf, trimmed, 6¹¹⁄₁₆ by 4³⁄₁₆ inches.
Issued in cloth, back lettered "The | British | Poets | Shelley | I."

Lowell was the author of the "Memoir of Shelley." Pp. [xvii]–xli. In this first edition it was unsigned, but in the 1857 edition Lowell's name was added and the copyright date was changed to 1857.

1855

The Boston Mob of "Gentlemen of Property and Standing." | [rule] | Proceedings | of the | Anti-Slavery Meeting | Held in Stacy Hall, Boston, on the | Twentieth Anniversary | of the | Mob of October 21, 1835. | [rule] | Phonographic Report by J. M. W. Yerrington. | [rule] | Boston: | Published by R. F. Wallcut. | 1855.

8vo. Collation: Title and imprint, pp. [1, 2]; text, pp. [3]–76. Size of leaf, trimmed, 9³⁄₁₆ by 5¾ inches.
Issued in paper covers, p. [1] printed from the types of the title-page, but enclosed in a double-rule frame; other cover pages blank.

A hymn by James Russell Lowell, beginning,

> "Friends of Freedom! ye who stand
> With no weapon in your hand,"

is found on p. 31. It was reprinted the next year on a broadside headed, "Anti-Slavery Festival | in Faneuil Hall. | A Welcome to Parker Pillsbury." It seems never to have been collected.

1855

The | Poems | of | Maria | Lowell. | [ornament] | Cambridge: | Privately Printed. | 1855.

12mo. Collation: Title, copyright (dated 1855) and imprint, Dedication, and Contents, pp. [i]–vi; text, pp. 1–68; Portrait, a "crystallotype" cut round and mounted, as frontispiece. Size of leaf, trimmed, 7¹⁄₁₆ by 5¹⁄₁₆ inches.

Issued in stamped cloth, gilt edges, back lettered "Poems."

Mrs. Lowell died October 27, 1853. This volume, of which fifty copies were printed for presentation to her friends, contains twenty poems only. The Dedication reads: "To | Emelyn Story, | Mary Lowell Putnam, | and | Sarah B. Shaw, | This book is dedicated."

The volume contains no writing of Lowell's, but it is so intimately associated with him that it is always one of the most prized items in a Lowell collection.

On May 25, 1854, Lowell wrote to E. A. Duyckinck: "I am about to print a little volume containing her poems—some of them never before printed. It is not to be published, but if you would like to make any use of it, I shall have great pleasure in sending you a copy."

On June 7 he wrote again: "With the little volume I spoke of in my last, you will find a very beautiful head. It is a *Crystallotype* of a drawing of Cheney's after a portrait by Page, and is like as far [as] there can be any likeness made of a face so full of spiritual beauty, and in which so much of the charm was subterficial."

And again on December 6: "My having been away from home all the summer has delayed the printing of the memorial volume I wrote to you about. It is now in the press and will be finished by January at farthest, I hope."

"Affection's Gift, A Christmas, New-Year and Birthday Present, for MDCCCLV.", Philadelphia, 1855, contains on p. 256, "Sonnet—Truth. By James Russell Lowell." This sonnet, with the title "Sub Pondere Crescit," appeared in "Poems," 1844, and later editions.

1857

[The Power of Sound.]

In the Introduction to the privately printed edition of "The Power of Sound" prepared by Mr. E. B. Holden in 1896, Prof. Charles Eliot Norton says:

"There are several references in it to incidents which occurred during the summer of 1857, from which it may be concluded that it was written in the autumn or early winter of that year; while other references in the additions show that the latest of them belong to the spring of 1862. The only existing copy of the poem is in print on galley slips, cut up so as to make twenty-three pages. The margins of many of these pages are full of corrections and additions written in ink or pencil. It was put into type and cut up into its present form for convenience of reading in public."

Once put in type and for a specific purpose, it is probable that more than a single copy was printed. One or more other copies may possibly still be in existence.

1857

The | Poetical Works | of | Andrew Marvell. | With a | Memoir of the Author. | [rule] | Boston: | Little, Brown and Company. | Shepard, Clark and Brown. | Cincinnati: Moore, Wilstach, Keys and Co. | M. DCCC. LVII.

16mo. Collation: Title, imprint, half-title, and Contents, pp. [i]–viii; Notice of the Author, pp. [ix]–liii; blank leaf, half-title, and text, pp. 1–335. Publishers' advertisements, 4 pp. bound in, in front. Size of leaf, trimmed, 6¾ by 4¼ inches.

Issued in cloth, back lettered "The | British | Poets | Marvell".

On December 6, 1854, Lowell wrote to E. A. Duyckinck: "You will be pleased I think, to hear that I have been editing Andrew Marvell's Poems for Little and Brown. I have spent a good deal of thought and labor on the text and it is not much to say that it will [be] the most correct yet. I am now at work upon Donne."

In the undated letter to his printer, Mr. Bolles, from which I have quoted on p. 44, he says:

[47]

Written in aid of the Fair for the Poor,

AT THE

BOSTON MUSIC HALL, MARCH, 1858.

———o———

AN AUTOGRAPH.

Though old the thought and oft expreſt,
'T is his at laſt who ſays it beſt,—
I'll try my fortune with the reſt.

Life is a leaf of paper white
Whereon each one of us may write
His word or two, and then comes night.

"Lo, time and ſpace enough," we cry,
"To write an epic!" ſo we try
Our nibs upon the edge and die.

Muſe not which way the pen to hold,
Luck hates the flow and loves the bold,
Soon come the darkneſs and the cold.

Greatly begin! though thou have time
But for a line, be that ſublime,—
Not failure, but low aim is crime.

Ah, with what lofty hope we came!
But we forget it, dream of fame,
And scrawl, as I do here, a name.

J. R. LOWELL.

Cambridge,
7th March, 1858.

[SIZE OF ORIGINAL]

[48]

"In the Marvell proof, p. xiv., will you be good enough to look at the life of Marvell in the 'Biographia Borealis' I left with you, & see if the date (1653) is right. I mean of M's appointment as Dutton's tutor. The date in the note is right—1657. There is a letter of M's about it in the Biographia which may be dated."

The book, however, seems not to have been published until 1857—at least I can find no copy with an earlier date. There is no copyright notice.

1857

The | Poetical Works | of | James R. Lowell. | Complete in two volumes. | Volume I. [Volume II.] | Boston: | Ticknor and Fields. | M DCCC LVIII.

2 vols., 18mo. Collation, Vol. I: Half-title, title, copyright (dated 1857) and imprint, Dedication, and Contents, pp. [i]–ix; text, pp. 1–315; portrait frontispiece. Vol. II: Half-title, title, copyright and imprint, Dedication, and Contents, pp. [i–vi]; text, pp. [vii]–322. Size of leaf, trimmed, 5½ by 3⁷⁄₁₆ inches.

Issued in blue cloth, gilt edges, back lettered "Lowell's | Poems | Vol I | Ticknor & Co".

The stereotype plates prepared for the two-volume edition of "Poems," 1849, were used without change for the printing of several editions, the last, marked "Seventh Edition" on the title-page, being issued in 1857. Later the same year, this two-volume edition in the "blue and gold" series was published. Vol. I contains all the poems of the 1849 edition with the exception of "Thistle-downs" and "The Morning Glory," the latter being by Mrs. Lowell. The pieces are differently arranged and a few slight changes were made in the titles of several. "Stanzas," pp. 205, 206 of the 1849 edition, here has the title "Stanzas on Freedom." Sonnet I is here addressed "To A. C. L." Sonnet VIII is here "To M. W., on her Birth-day." In the earlier editions it had been "To ——, on her Birth-day." Sonnet XX, formerly entitled simply "To ——," is here "To M. O. S."

Vol. II contains four poems: 1. "A Fable for Critics," with rhymed title-page, having the date of publication "October, the 31st day." 2. "The Biglow Papers." 3. "The Unhappy Lot of Mr. Knott." 4. "An Oriental Apologue." No. 3 was first printed in *Graham's Magazine* for April, 1851, and No. 4 in the *Anti-Slavery Standard* for April 12, 1849. Both are here first collected in book-form.

TO

MR. JOHN BARTLETT.

ON SENDING ME A SEVEN-POUND TROUT.

———◆———

FIT for an Abbot of Theleme,
    For the whole Cardinals' College, or
The Pope himself to see in dream
Before his lenten vision gleam,
He lies there, the sogdologer!

His precious flanks with stars besprent,
Worthy to swim in Castaly!
The friend by whom such gifts are sent,
For him shall bumpers full be spent,
His health! be Luck his fast ally!

PAGE I OF LEAFLET "TO JOHN BARTLETT"

[SIZE OF ORIGINAL]

1858

Written in aid of the Fair for the Poor, | at the | Boston Music Hall, March, 1858. | [rule] | An Autograph. | [text, six stanzas of three lines each] | J. R. Lowell. | Cambridge, | 7th March, 1858.

16mo. 2 leaves. The above printed on p. [1]; pp. 2–4 blank. Size of leaf, 6¼ by 3⅞ inches.

This poem was reprinted in "Under the Willows," 1868, with title, "For an Autograph." The only copy of the leaflet I can trace belongs to Mr. Stephen H. Wakeman.

1858

To | Mr. John Bartlett. | On sending me a seven-pound trout. |

12mo. 2 leaves. The above at the top of p. [1]; 2 stanzas, 5 lines each, on p. [1]; 3 stanzas each on pp. [2] and [3], and 2 stanzas on p. [4]. Signed "J. R. Lowell", and dated "Elmwood, 1858." Size of leaf, 6⅝ by 5 inches.

It is with some uncertainty that I insert this leaflet under the date 1858. The trout was certainly sent and the poem *written* in that year, though it was not published until 1866, when it appeared in the *Atlantic Monthly* for July. On May 30, 1866, Lowell wrote to Charles Eliot Norton: "You will see my verses to Bartlett in the next *Atlantic,* and I guess you will like 'em. They seemed to me fanciful and easy when I corrected the proof, with some droll triple rhymes."

Norton was one of his closest friends and nearest neighbors, yet this reads as if the poem were a new one, and unfamiliar.

We know that Bartlett reprinted the poem in 1882 as a single quarto leaf for insertion in copies of his "Catalogue of Books on Angling" published in that year. It there bears the same date at end, "Elmwood, 1858," as appears upon this rarer and earlier four-page leaflet. As Bartlett was a collector of books on fishing, we may presume that, upon receipt of the manuscript from his friend, he at once had it put into type and a few copies struck off. At least, until we know something more definite of its origin, we can only put it under the date it bears. I know of only a single copy.

ALL SAINTS.

One Feast, of holy days the crest,
  I, though no churchman, love to keep,
All Saints—the unknown good that rest
  In God's still memory folded deep ;
The bravely dumb that did their deed,
  And scorned to blot it with a name,
Men of the plain heroic breed,
  That loved Heaven's silence more than fame.

Such lived not in the past alone,
  But thread to-day the unheeding street,
And stairs to Sin and Famine known,
  Sing with the welcome of their feet ;
The den they enter grows a shrine,
  The grimy sash an oriel burns,
Their cup of water warms like wine,
  Their speech is filled from heavenly urns.

About their brows to me appears
  An aureole traced in tenderest light,
The rainbow-gleam of smiles through tears
  In dying eyes, by them made bright,
Of souls that shivered on the edge
  Of that chill ford repassed no more,
And in their mercy felt the pledge
  And sweetness of the farther shore.

                  J. R. LOWELL.

Written for Harriet Ryan's Fair.
March 20th, 1859.

[SIZE OF ORIGINAL]

[52]

The quarto leaflet has been described as a first edition, but this is impossible, as from its form we know that it was printed in 1882 to accompany Bartlett's "Catalogue."

The poem was collected by Lowell in "Under the Willows," 1868.

1858

Report | of | The Committee | of the | Association of the Alumni | of | Harvard College, | Appointed to take into consideration | The State of the College Library, | In Accordance with a vote of the Association passed | at the Annual Meeting July 16, 1857. | [rule] | Cambridge: | Metcalf and Company, | Printers to the University. | 1858.

8vo. Collation: Title and text, pp. [1]–44. Size of leaf, trimmed, 8⅞ by 5⅞ inches.

Issued in paper cover, the first page printed from the types of the title-page.

A "Statement of Professor Lowell" is found on pp. 20, 21. It has never been reprinted.

1858

Poetry of the Bells | collected by | Samuel Batchelder, Jr | [vignette] | Riverside Press | Printed in aid of the Cambridge Chime | By H. O. Houghton and Company | 1858

12mo. Collation: Title, quotation (6 lines), and Contents, pp. [1]–4; text, pp. [5–72]. Size of leaf, trimmed, 7½ by 4⅞ inches.

Issued in stamped cloth, red edges, back lettered "Poetry | of the | Bells".

This volume contains a poem especially written for the occasion: "Godminster Chimes." Signed and dated at end "J. R. Lowell. | Dec. 9, 1858." Pp. 57–60.

It was collected in "Under the Willows," 1868. "An Incident of the Fire at Hamburg," which had appeared in "Poems," second series, 1848, is also included in the volume.

1859

All Saints. | [rule] | [text, three stanzas of eight lines each] | J. R. Lowell. | Written for Harriet Ryan's Fair. | March 20th, 1859.

16mo. A single sheet, printed on one side only, as above. Size of sheet, 6¼ by 4 inches.

The only specimen of this leaflet which I have been able to trace is the one in the library of Harvard University. The poem was collected in "Under the Willows," 1868.

1859

The | Biglow Papers. | By | James Russell Lowell. | Newly Edited, | With a Preface | By the | Author of "Tom Brown's School-Days." | Reprinted, | With the Author's Sanction, | from the Fourth American Edition. | London: | Trübner & Co. 60, Paternoster Row. | 1859.

16mo. Collation: Half-title, title, imprint, Publishers' Preface, English Editor's Preface, Contents, Notices of an Independent Press, half-title, half-title, Note, and Introduction, pp. [i–lxviii]; text, Glossary, and Index, pp. [1]–140. Size of leaf, 6¾ by 5 inches.

Issued in cloth, back lettered "The | Biglow | Papers | Lowell | Trübner & Co."

This edition, though otherwise interesting, finds a place here solely on account of the letter from Lowell incorporated in the "Publishers' Preface." This letter is dated "Cambridge, Massachusetts, 14th September, 1859," and is as follows:

FIRST EDITIONS OF LOWELL

"I think it would be well for you to announce that you are to publish an Authorized Edition of the 'Biglow Papers'; for I have just received a letter from Mr. —— who tells me that a Mr. —— was thinking of an edition, and wished him to edit it. Any such undertaking will be entirely against my will, and I take it for granted that Mr. —— only formed the plan in ignorance of your intention.

"With many thanks, very truly yours,

"J. R. LOWELL."

The unauthorized edition referred to by Lowell appeared almost simultaneously with this one. It has the title:

The Choicest Humorous Poetry of the Age. | [waved rule] | The | Biglow Papers, | By | James Russell Lowell. | [rule] | Alluded to by John Bright in the House of Commons. | [rule] | With | Additional Notes, an enlarged Glossary, | and | an Illustration by George Cruikshank. | London: | John Camden Hotten, | Piccadilly | [rule] | 1859.

The Preface, signed "John Camden Hotten," is dated "Piccadilly, Oct. 25, 1859." The "Additional Notes" are signed "J. C. H."

In the "Letters," Vol. I, pp. 275, 276, Professor Norton prints a letter from Lowell to Sydney Howard Gay, dated "Cambridge, Dec. 21, 1856," containing the following statements:

"MY DEAR SYDNEY,—Your having edited a pirated edition of the 'Biglow Papers' puts me in mind of what happened to a classmate of mine. . . . But never mind, I sha'n't lose much by it, and even if I should, I should be willing to pay something for the amusement of seeing on the title-page that the book had been 'alluded to by Mr. Bright in Parliament.' Only think of it! it quite takes my breath away. But better yet, what foretaste of immortality like being edited with philological notes? It makes me feel as if the grass were growing over me."

This seems to show that Gay had something to do with the preparation of this edition. The date 1856 should, without much doubt, be 1859.

1859

Celebration | of the | Hundredth Anniversary | of the | Birth of Robert Burns, | By the | Boston Burns Club. | January 25th, 1859. | [rule] | Boston: | Printed by H. W. Dutton and Son, | Transcript Building. | 1859.

[55]

12mo. Collation: Title and text, pp. [1]–84. Size of leaf, trimmed, 7⁷⁄₁₆ by 4¹⁵⁄₁₆ inches.

Issued in cloth, front cover lettered "Boston Burns Club. | Centennial Festival, | 1859."

Lowell's contribution to this volume has the title: "Poem of James Russell Lowell, Esq."

"A hundred years! they 're quickly fled."

Pp. 55–59. It was not collected until 1888, when it was included in the "Heartsease and Rue" volume, under the title "At the Burns Centennial." Mr. Chamberlain acquired the original of Lowell's letter of acceptance to attend the meeting of the Club. It is as follows:

"I have the honor to acknowledge your kind invitation to the 'Burns Festival.' I shall come with great pleasure and shall have my contribution to the festivities ready if there shall be room for it."

1859

Gifts of Genius: | A Miscellany | of | Prose and Poetry, | By | American Authors. | [ornament] | New York: | Printed for C. A. Davenport.

12mo. Collation: Half-title, title, copyright (dated 1859), Contents, To the Public, and Introductory, pp. [i]–xii; text, pp. 13–264. Size of leaf, trimmed, 7½ by 5 inches.

Issued in stamped cloth, gilt edges, back lettered "Gifts | of | Genius".

This volume, which was edited by William Cullen Bryant, and privately printed for Miss C. A. Davenport, a blind school-teacher of New York, contains "Sea-Weed. | By James Russell Lowell." Pp. 89, 90. This was collected in "Under the Willows.", 1869.

Lowell contributed the article "Dante" to the first edition of Appleton's American Encyclopædia, published from 1857 to 1863, the volume containing the "Dante" appearing in 1859. It was reprinted in 1886 in the "Fifth Annual Report of the Dante Society."

"The Bobolink Minstrel; or, Republican Songster, for 1860" contains, on p. 34, Lowell's "The Present Crisis." This had appeared in "Poems," 1848.

1861

Favorite Authors. | A Companion-Book | of | Prose and Poetry. | My Books, my best companions. | Fletcher | [device] | Boston: | Ticknor and Fields. | M DCCC LXI.

12mo. Collation: Title, copyright (dated 1860) and imprint, and Contents, pp. [i]–iv; text, pp. [1]–[300]. Plates, separately printed, facing title and pp. 21, 27, 37, 45, 66, 71, 89, 91, 106, 109, 123, 131, 145, 159, 161, 184, 189, 211, 216, 240, 249, 265, 270, 294. Size of leaf, trimmed, 7½ by 5 inches.

Issued in cloth, back lettered "Favorite | Authors | Ticknor & Co."

This volume contains "Cambridge Worthies—Thirty Years Ago. | By James Russell Lowell." Pp. [270]–293.
This had appeared in *Putnam's Monthly* for April and May, 1853. When collected in "Fireside Travels" in 1864, the title was altered to "Cambridge Thirty Years Ago."

1861

The | Victoria Regia: | A volume of | Original Contributions in Poetry and Prose. | Edited by | Adelaide A. Procter. | [device] | London: | Printed and Published by Emily Faithfull and Co., | Victoria Press, (for the Employment of Women,) | Great Coram Street, W. C. | 1861. | Entered at Stationers' Hall.

8vo. Collation: Title, illustration, Dedication, Preface, Contents, pp. [i]–x; half-title and text, pp. [1]–349. Imprint, p. [350]. Size of leaf, trimmed, 9 by 6¼ inches.

Issued in stamped cloth, gilt edges, back lettered "The | Victoria | Regia | London. 1861". Also in stamped morocco.

This volume, to which Thackeray, Tennyson, Matthew Arnold, and others were also contributors, contains "The Fatal Curiosity.", signed at end "J. R. Lowell." Pp. 83, 84. It seems never to have been reprinted.

[57]

IL PESCEBALLO.

OPERA SERIA: IN UN ATTO.

MUSICA DEL MAESTRO ROSSIBELLI-DONIMOZARTI.

PERSONAGGI.

Lo STRANIERO *(Tenore)*.

IL CAMERIERE *(Basso)*

LA PADRONA *(Soprano)*

Un Corriere, Serve della Locanda, Studenti di Padova.

La Scena è in Padova.

[* *Il Pesceballo* (corruzione della voce inglese *Fish-ball*) è un prodotto della cucina americana, consistente in una combinazione di stoccofisso con patate, fatta nella forma di pallottole, simili alle nostre polpette, e poi fritta. Msgr. Bedini, nel suo *Viaggio negli Stati Uniti,* c' insegna che la detta pietanza si usa massimamente nella Nuova-Inghilterra, ove, secondo quel venerabile autore, viene specialmente mangiato a colazione nelle domeniche.]

[SIZE OF ORIGINAL]

1862

From the Atlantic Monthly. | Mason and Slidell: A Yankee Idyll. | To the Editors of the Atlantic Monthly. | Jaalam, 6ᵗʰ Jan., 1862. | Gentlemen,—I was highly gratified by the insertion of a portion of my letter in the last | [etc.]

8vo. Collation: No title-page; above at top of p. 1. Letter, signed "Homer Wilbur, A.M.", pp. 1–2; Poem, pp. 3–12; lower half of p. 12 blank. Head-lines of pp. 2, 4, 6, 8, and 10 are: "Mason and Slidell: A Yankee Idyll. [February," and of pp. 3, 5, 7, 9, and 11: "1862] Mason and Slidell: A Yankee Idyll." Head-line of p. 12: "Reviews and Literary Notices. [February,". Size of leaf, untrimmed, 9⅝ by 6¹⁄₁₆ inches.

Issued stitched, without cover.

"Mason and Slidell," the second of the "Biglow Papers, Second Series," appeared in the *Atlantic Monthly* for February, 1862. This separate issue was printed from the types of the magazine, with slight typographical alterations. The words "From the Atlantic Monthly", at the top of the first page, do not occur in the magazine, the pages of which are numbered 259–270 instead of 1–12. The lower half of the last page in the magazine contains the beginning of the next article, "Reviews and Literary Notices."

Just how many copies of this separate issue were printed cannot now be traced. Seven or eight copies are now known—a large number when the fragile nature of the pamphlet is considered. No mention of it seems to have been made in the published letters, and, so far as we know, none of the other "Papers" were separately printed from the magazine types.

1862

Il Pesceballo. | [rule] | Opera Seria: in un Atto. | Musica del Maestro Rossibelli-Donimozarti. | [rule] | Personaggi. | Lo Straniero (Tenore). | Il Cameriere (Basso). | La Padrona (Soprano). | Un Corriere, Serve della Locanda, Studenti di Padova. | [rule] |

La Scena è in Padova. | [rule] | [8 lines] | [Boston, 1862.]

16mo. Collation: No title-page, above heading being on p. [1];
text, pp. 2–31. Size of leaf, trimmed, 6^{15}⁄$_{16}$ by 4½ inches.
Issued stitched, without cover.

Mr. Chamberlain was the first to discover that there were actually
three distinct editions of this scarce pamphlet, differing only in minor
typographical particulars. This first edition was printed as an octavo on
four sheets, with signature marks "1", "2", "3", and "4" on pp. [1], 9, 17,
and 25 respectively. The paper used was a "wove" paper, without wire-
marks or chain-lines. The second and third editions were printed on
"laid" paper, on two sheets, with two signature marks only, "1" and "2",
on pp. [1] and 17. The first and second editions were issued without covers. The third edition has a tea-green printed paper cover, with title
enclosed within a double rule: "Il Pesceballo | Opera | in un Atto |
Musica del Maestro Rossibelli-Donimozarti | [ornament] | Cambridge |
Printed at the Riverside Press | 1862."

The following are typographical points of difference noted by him:

The signature marks on pp. [1] and 17 in the third edition are in a
larger type than those of the second edition.

P. 4, l. 4: "piacier" in first edition is corrected to "piacer" in second
and third editions.

P. 5, last line: "Saloon" is in roman type in first edition; in italic type
in second and third.

P. 8, l. 1: "pocco" in the first edition is corrected to "poco" in second
and third.

P. 18, l. 4: "più" in first and third editions is "piú" in second.

P. 18, l. 8: "anchorè" in first edition is corrected to "ancorchè" in the
second and third.

P. 23, l. 10: "and" is italic type in the first and second editions; roman
in the third.

P. 30, last line: "Fine del Pesceballo." in the first and second editions
measures full 1⅜ inches in length, while in the third edition, being printed
in a slightly smaller type, it measures only a hair's-breadth more than 1¼
inches.

Although Mr. Chamberlain called these three forms first, second, and
third issues, I am confident that the types were actually set three times
and that they are more accurately described as first, second, and third
editions. For the most part, they seem to have been printed from the
same font of type, and set in the same office, perhaps by the same com-
positor. There are sufficient differences in measurements, relative posi-
tions of lines, broken types, position of accents, and different forms of
marks of punctuation (especially the exclamation-point and parenthesis)
to make it improbable that the types were kept standing while two even
of the three editions were printed.

Mr. Chamberlain made an effort to discover just when the first public performance of the opera was given. He has transcribed a letter from Prof. Child in which he says that "the Fishball opera (Il Pesceballo) was printed for a series of performances in Cambridge in the Spring of 1862." Mr. Wakeman's copy of the second edition has a pencil memorandum: "Given at house of Miss Parsons, Garden St. May 6, 1862." With this as a guide, Mr. Chamberlain visited the family of Miss Parsons in December, 1902, and saw in their possession a copy of the book (also second edition) with inscription: "Emily Parsons | May 1862 Cambridge."

At the earlier performances, at least, the tenor part was taken by Dr. W. Langmaid, the basso by Mr. Underwood, and the soprano by Mrs. Benjamin Apthorp Gould.

The reprint published in 1899 by the Caxton Club of Chicago was made from a copy of the third edition. It contains an Introduction by Charles Eliot Norton:

"This *jeu d'esprit* was written in Italian by Francis James Child and was sung frequently in Boston and vicinity during the later years of the Civil War, the proceeds being turned over to Edward Everett for his fund for the relief of the loyal people of East Tennessee who had been impoverished by the war. The proceeds of later performances may have been used for other charities.

"The verso of each leaf contains Prof. Child's Italian text, while Lowell's translation into English is on the recto of the next leaf, facing it. This translation, no doubt considered by him of the most ephemeral character, is not included in any of the collected editions of Lowell's works."

Laid in Mr. Chamberlain's copy was a letter from Charles Eliot Norton, dated April 4, 1902, in which he says: " 'Il Pesceballo' was originally issued in brown covers." This is undoubtedly a mistake. The earlier copies were issued without covers, and no copy of any edition with a brown cover can be traced.

1862

The | Biglow Papers. | By | James Russell Lowell. | Second Series. | Part I. Containing | 1. Birdofredum Sawin, Esq. to Mr. Hosea Biglow. | 2. Mason and Slidell: A Yankee Idyll. | Authorized Edition. | London: | Trübner & Co. 60, Paternoster Row. | 1862.

12mo. Collation: Title, p. [1]; imprint, "London: | R. Clay, Son, and Taylor, Printers, | Bread Street Hill." p. [2]; text, pp. [3]–52, with imprint "R. Clay, Son, and Taylor, Printers, London."

THE

BIGLOW PAPERS.

BY

JAMES RUSSELL LOWELL.

SECOND SERIES.

PART I. CONTAINING

1. BIRDOFREDUM SAWIN, ESQ. TO MR. HOSEA BIGLOW.
2. MASON AND SLIDELL: A YANKEE IDYLL.

𝔄𝔲𝔱𝔥𝔬𝔯𝔦𝔷𝔢𝔡 𝔈𝔡𝔦𝔱𝔦𝔬𝔫.

LONDON:
TRÜBNER & CO. 60, PATERNOSTER ROW.
1862.

[SIZE OF ORIGINAL]

at bottom of p. 52.   Size of leaf, 7³⁄₁₆ by 4¹⁵⁄₁₆ inches.   Edges trimmed, but top uncut and unopened.

Issued in unglazed pink paper covers. P. [1] printed from the types of the title-page and enclosed within a single-rule frame. Below the rule is "Price One Shilling." P. [2] contains advertisements of "The Biglow Papers" and "Reynard the Fox"; p. [3], of "Baron Munchausen" and "Master Tyll Owlglass"; and p. [4], of the "Strange, Surprising Adventures of the Venerable Gooroo Simple."

The book consists of signatures A, B, C, each 8 ll., and D, 2 ll., title leaf being A.   There are signature marks on A2, B, B2, C, C2, and D.

The first of these two pieces appeared in the *Atlantic Monthly* for January, 1862, and the second, as already noted, in the number for February, 1862.

1862

The | Biglow Papers. | By | James Russell Lowell. | Second Series. | Part II. Containing | 1. Birdofredum Sawin, Esq. to Mr. Hosea Biglow. | 2. A Message of Jeff Davis in Secret Session. | Authorized Edition. | London: | Trübner & Co. 60, Paternoster Row. | 1862.

12mo. Collation: Title, p. [i]; imprint, "London: | R. Clay, Son, and Taylor, Printers, | Bread Street Hill.", p. [ii]; text, pp. [53]–90, with imprint "R. Clay, Son, and Taylor, Printers, Bread Street Hill." at the bottom of p. [90]. Size of leaf, trimmed throughout, 6⅞ by 4¹³⁄₁₆ inches.

Issued in unglazed pink paper covers. P. [1] printed from the types of the title-page and enclosed in a single-rule frame. Above the rule is "Originally published in the Atlantic Monthly." (this line is not on the cover of Part I), and below the rule, "Price One Shilling." Pp. 2, 3, and 4 of cover are identical with those of Part I.

The book consists of signatures E, F, each 8 ll., and G, 4 ll. Title leaf is E.   There are signature marks on E2, F, and G.

These two pieces appeared first in the *Atlantic Monthly* for March and April, 1862.

1862

The | Biglow Papers. | By | James Russell Lowell. | Second Series. | Part III. Containing | 1. Speech of Honourable Preserved Doe in | Secret Caucus. | 2. Suthin' in the Pastoral Line. | Authorized Edition. | London: | Trübner & Co. 60, Paternoster Row. | 1862.

12mo. Collation: Title, p. [i]; imprint, "London: | R. Clay, Son, and Taylor, Printers, | Bread Street Hill.", p. [ii]; text, pp. [91]–120. No imprint on p. 120. Size of leaf, trimmed, 6¹¹⁄₁₆ by 4⅞ inches.

Issued in unglazed pink paper covers. P. [1] printed from the types of the title, enclosed in a single-rule frame. Inscriptions above and below the frame as in Part II. Pp. 2, 3, and 4 of cover as in Parts I and II.

The book consists of signatures H and I, each 8 ll. Title leaf is H. Signature marks on H2 (wrongly printed H), I, and I2.

These two pieces appeared in the *Atlantic Monthly* for May and June, 1862. It is remarkable how popular the "Biglow Papers" seems to have been in England. These three thin pamphlets, as well as other editions published by Trübner & Co., to be noted later, appeared there many months before the magazine articles were collected by their author.

It is not likely that the three parts appeared simultaneously, for, as will be seen, as soon as additional pieces (which might have formed a Part IV) appeared, the whole was collected into one volume. The copies of Parts I, II, and III in the British Museum were received there on August 9, 1862.

1862

[Rule] | Only Once. | Original Papers, by various Contributors. | Published for the Benefit of the New York Infirmary for Women and Children. | No. 126 Second Avenue. 1862. | [rule] | Contributors: |

C. M. Sedgwick.	Wm. Cullen Bryant.	Geo. H. Boker.
C. M. Kirkland.	John G. Whittier.	Theodore Tilton.
E. A. Stoddard.	O. B. Frothingham.	E. J. Cutler.
Phoebe Carey.	James Russell Lowell.	Charles Eliot Norton.
Edna Dean Proctor.	Charles T. Brooks.	T. R.
Rose Terry.	Bayard Taylor.	S. L.
Marie E. Fellowes.	William Page.	

| Music: Whittier's song of the Negro Boatman at Port Royal. | [rule] | Price, 25 Cents. | Or, with engraved Portraits of Bryant and Lowell, and Miss Sedgwick, and View of Florence, price 50 Cents. | [rule] | John F. Trow, Printer, 50 Greene Street.

4to. Collation: Title, Note of Committee and copyright (dated 1862), pp. [1–2]; text, pp. [3]–15. Portraits, separately printed, facing pp. 5, 6, and 8, and plate facing p. 11. Size of leaf, untrimmed, 11¾ by 9⅜ inches.

Issued stitched, without covers.

This pamphlet contains a poem, "Before the Embers. | By James Russell Lowell." P. 6. It was apparently never reprinted.

The copy described above is of the variety published at "50 Cents" with three portraits and one plate.

1864

No. 16. | The President's Policy | By | James Russell Lowell. | From the North American Review, January, 1864. | [Philadelphia, 1864.]

8vo. Collation: No title-page, above being first page of cover; text, pp. [1]–22; pp. [23, 24] blank. Size of leaf, trimmed, 8¹³⁄₁₆ by 5¹³⁄₁₆ inches.

Issued in paper cover. P. [1] as above, enclosed within an ornamental border. Pp. [2] and [3] of the cover contain an extract, "The Northern Message," reprinted from the London *Spectator* of December 26. P. [4] contains an advertisement of the *North American Review*.

Beginning with the number for January, 1864, the editorship of the *North American Review* was taken up by James Russell Lowell and Charles Eliot Norton, and to the first number Lowell contributed this article, "The President's Policy," being a review of President Lincoln's message to Congress dated December 9, 1863. This reprint of the article (from a new setting of type) was made for the Union League Club of Philadelphia. The "No. 16" on the cover indicates, probably, its order in the series of political tracts printed for the Club. It was probably published in March, and the printers were probably Crissy & Markley, who printed other pamphlets of the series.

Lincoln read the article and wrote to the publishers of the *Review*: "Of course I am not the most impartial judge; yet, with due allowance for this, I venture to hope that the article entitled 'The President's Policy' will be of value to the country. I fear I am not quite worthy of all which is therein kindly said of me personally." He goes on to say of a sentence at the top of page 252, that he could wish it "to be not exactly as it is." In consequence of this remark there is an editorial note of two lines at the bottom of p. 15 of the pamphlet, which was not in the magazine article. In the first line of text, the word "crises" in the magazine was changed to "crisises" in the pamphlet.

An extended account of the pamphlet was contributed by Theodore Wesley Koch to *The Bibliographer* for February, 1903.

1864

Fireside Travels. | By | James Russell Lowell. | [quotation, 4 lines] | [publishers' device] | Boston: | Ticknor and Fields. | 1864.

12mo. Collation: Blank, p. [1]; list of Lowell's writings, p. [2]; title, copyright (dated 1864) and imprint, Dedication, Note, and Contents, pp. [i–vii]; half-title and text, pp. 1–324. Size of leaf, trimmed, 7⅛ by 4½ inches.

Issued in stamped cloth, back lettered "Fireside | Travels | Lowell | Ticknor & Co."

As the author says in his note on p. [v], the greater part of this volume had appeared ten years before in *Putnam's Monthly* and *Graham's Magazine*. These pieces are: "Cambridge Thirty Years Ago" and "A Moosehead Journal." The first had been reprinted in the volume "Favorite Authors," as already noted. The remainder of the book, "Letters from my Journal in Italy and Elsewhere," was "selected from old letters and journals written on the spot." The volume was published in April or

May, 1864, and Mr. Chamberlain was of the opinion that the first issue was sent out without publishers' list. Later issues have a list dated September, 1864 (or later date), bound in at the end.

1864

The Spirit of the Fair 1864 | "None But the Brave deserve the Fair" | Tuesday, | April 5, 1864. | Editorial Committee: | Augustus R. Macdonough, Chairman. | Mrs. Charles E. Butler, Mrs. Edward Cooper, | C. Astor Bristed, Chester P. Dewey, James W. Gerard, Jr., William J. Hoppin, Henry D. Sedgwick, | Frederick Sheldon, Charles K. Tuckerman. | John F. Trow, Publisher and Printer, 50. Greene St. New York. |

4to. Collation: Pp. [1–208]. Consists of seventeen numbers or parts, issued daily (except Sundays) from April 5 to April 23, 1864. Each number consists of title, 1 p.; advertisements, 1 p.; text, 8 pp., and advertisements, 2 pp., except the last number, which has 12 pp. of text. Although included in the pagination, the first and last leaves of each number actually formed a cover. Each number (except the second) was copyrighted by Augustus R. Macdonough.

This paper was published during the continuance of the Metropolitan Fair of the Sanitary Commission held at New York, April 5 to April 23, 1864. The number for Tuesday, April 12, contains "To a Friend who sent me a Meerschaum. | By James Russell Lowell." Pp. 79, 80. The poem was not collected until 1888, when it was included in the "Heartsease and Rue" volume, but with the altered title: "To C. F. Bradford, on the Gift of a Meerschaum Pipe."
Later in the year the stereotype plates were purchased by John F. Trow. A general title, "The | Spirit of the Fair. | [8 lines] | New York: | John F. Trow, Publisher, 50 Greene Street.", and a leaf, "Publisher's Notice," were prefixed, and the whole issued in one volume, bound in boards. The covers of the numbers were not included, so that there is a gap of four pages between each two numbers. A "Report of the Treasurer of the Metropolitan Fair" is bound in at the end.

1864

Autograph Leaves of Our Country's Authors. | [Vignette] | Baltimore, | Cushings & Bailey | 1864.

4to. Collation: Blank, p. [i]; copyright (dated 1864) and imprint, title, Preface, and Contents, pp. [ii]–xi; text, pp. 1–200; vignette, p. [201]. Size of leaf, trimmed, 10¼ by 8½ inches.

Issued in smooth, stamped cloth, back lettered "Autograph | Leaves | of our | Country's | Authors."

This curious volume, lithographed throughout, consists of a series of reproductions of manuscripts of American authors. Lowell's contribution was "The Courtin'," filling pp. 107–112, signed at end "J. R. Lowell." This dialect poem had appeared among the "Notices of an Independent Press," in the first series of "Biglow Papers," 1848. In Lowell's own words (from his Introduction to "The Biglow Papers, Second Series," 1867):

"While the Introduction to the First Series was going through the press, I received word from the printer that there was a blank page left which must be filled. I sat down at once and improvised another fictitious 'notice of the press,' in which, because verse would fill up space more cheaply than prose, I inserted an extract from a supposed ballad of Mr. Biglow. I kept no copy of it, and the printer, as directed, cut it off when the gap was filled. Presently I began to receive letters asking for the rest of it, sometimes for the *balance* of it. I had none, but to answer such demands, I patched a conclusion upon it in a later edition. Those who had only the first continued to importune me. Afterwards, being asked to write it out as an autograph for the Baltimore Sanitary Commission Fair, I added other verses, into some of which I infused a little more sentiment in a homely way, and after a fashion completed it by sketching in the characters and making a connected story. Most likely I have spoiled it, but I shall put it at the end of this Introduction, to answer once for all those kindly importunings."

1864

The | Biglow Papers. | By | James Russell Lowell. | Second Series. | Authorized Edition. | London: | Trübner & Co. 60, Paternoster Row. | 1864.

12mo. Collation: Title, p. [i]; imprint, "London: | R. Clay, Son, and Taylor, Printers, | Bread Street Hill.", p. [ii]; Contents, p.

[1]; blank, p. [2]; text, pp. [3]–133, with imprint, "R. Clay, Son, and Taylor, Printers, London.", at bottom of p. 133; blank, p. [134]. Size of leaf, trimmed, 6⅝ by 4¾ inches.

Issued in unglazed pink paper covers. P. [1] printed from the types of the title, but enclosed in a single-rule frame. No legend above or below the rule. Pp. 2 and 3 with "paste-downs." P. 4, advertisement of "The Biglow Papers. First Series."

The book consists of title and Contents, 2 ll. without signature mark; signatures A, 7 ll. (lacking A); B, C, each 8 ll.; D, 2 ll.; E, 7 ll. (lacking E); F, 8 ll.; G, 4 ll.; H, 7 ll. (lacking H); I, 8 ll.; K, 8 ll., the last blank and used as a paste-down. There are signature marks on A2, B, B2, C, C2, D, E2, F, G, H2 (wrongly printed H), I, I2, K, and K2.

These are the identical sheets of the three original parts with a new title-page and additional leaves, the old title-pages (A1, E1, and H1) to the separate parts being torn out. The imprints occur on pp. 52 and 90.

In two copies examined the "stab-holes" are evident in Part II, showing that it had been bound. In one, fragments of the pink paper cover of that part are discoverable. The additional leaves (pp. 90–133) contain "Latest Views of Mr. Biglow," which appeared in the *Atlantic Monthly* for February, 1863. The copy in the British Museum was acquired on November 2, 1864.

There was a second printing from the same plates, differing typographically only in that the imprints on pp. 52 and 90 do not appear, having been cut from the plates. The imprint still is found on p. 133. This second edition appeared in glazed pink paper covers. The plates were again used the next year, but resignatured for more economical printing. This issue, dated 1865, consists of the title-page (1 leaf) without signature, and signatures A, B, C, D, E, F, G, and H, each 8 ll. and I, 4 ll., the last blank and used as a paste-down. In the earlier editions the title was A. Here the Contents leaf is the first leaf of the signature, and has the signature mark "A." This was also published in glazed paper covers.

An edition of "The Biglow Papers" containing the First Series complete, and Nos. I to VII of the Second Series, was published in London by S. O. Beeton late in 1865, though in the copy seen the title-page is undated. It has no first-edition value, though it antedated American publication of the Second Series as a book by about a year.

1864

Memorial | R G S [as a monogram] | Cambridge | University Press | 1864 |.

4to. Collation: Title, p. [i]; blank, p. [ii]; text, pp. 1–195; imprint, "University Press: | Welch, Bigelow, and Company, |

Cambridge.", p. [196]. Photographic frontispiece. Size of leaf, untrimmed, 9⅛ by 7 inches.

Issued in half leather, paper sides, back lettered "Memorial | R. G. S."

This volume contains Lowell's memorial verses to Colonel Robert Gould Shaw, "Memoriae Positum," signed "James Russell Lowell." Pp. 188–191. Also a letter written to Colonel Shaw's mother, dated "August 28, 1863" and signed "'J. R. Lowell." Pp. 148, 149. This letter is published by Mr. Norton (Vol. I, pp. 327, 328), but I may quote the following passage:

"I have been writing something about Robert, and if, after keeping a little while, it should turn out to be a poem, I shall print it,—but not unless I think it some way worthy of what I feel, however far the best verse falls short of noble living and dying such as his.".

He kept the poem by him until November 30, 1863, when he sent it to James T. Fields, saying: "I want to fling my leaf on dear Shaw's grave." It was first printed in the *Atlantic Monthly* for January, 1864, and afterwards collected in "Under the Willows," 1868.

Of this handsome volume, printed at the expense of the Shaw family, but very few copies were printed, and it is one of the rarest of first editions of Lowell.

1864

The | Bryant Festival | at | "The Century," | November 5, M.DCCC.LXIV. | New York: | D. Appleton and Company, | 443 & 445 Broadway. | M.DCCC.LXV.

8vo. Collation: Title, copyright ('dated 1864), pp. [1–2]; text, pp. [3]–88. Size of leaf, trimmed, 8⅜ by 6⅛ inches.

Issued in lavender boards, front lettered in red "The | Bryant Festival | at | "The Century." 150 copies were printed on large paper and bound in half roan, gilt top. These contain twenty-two portraits and two other engravings, separately printed and inserted. Size of leaf, 11⅞ by 9⅜ inches.

On p. 59 is "Extract of Mr. James R. Lowell's Letter." and his poem to Bryant follows: "On Board the Seventy-Six. | By James Russell Lowell." Pp. 59–61.

1864

[The Old Dramatists.]

[70]

Mr. Scudder, in his "James Russell Lowell, A Biography," Vol. II, p. 78, prints the following as a foot-note:

"An interesting venture was made by Little, Brown & Co. in the summer of 1864, which unfortunately proved too uncertain to be carried through. Lowell was to have edited a series of volumes illustrative of the Old Dramatists, from Marlowe down. He prepared one volume, which was put into type but never published. A set of proofs is in the library of Harvard University."

Mr. Norton, in the "Letters," Vol. I, p. 359, referring to the same undertaking, says: "A single volume was printed but not published."

It is probable that Mr. Scudder's statement is the more accurate and that the volume never got beyond the proof-sheet stage. It is possible, however, that more than a single set has been preserved.

Lowell is given as one of the "Editorial Council" of "The Boatswain's Whistle," published at the National Sailors' Fair in Boston in 1864, but he seems to have contributed nothing to the paper. Ten numbers were published, dated November 9, 10, 11, 12, 14, 15, 16, 17, 18, and 19. The Editor was Julia Ward Howe, and the "Editorial Council" consisted of Edward Everett, John G. Whittier, O. W. Holmes, A. P. Peabody, J. R. Lowell, and E. P. Whipple.

The "History of the Great Western Sanitary Fair," published in Cincinnati in 1864 (though the title-page is undated), contains, on pp. 183, 184, a short letter from Lowell dated "Cambridge, Dec. 19, 1863."

1865

Ode | Recited at the | Commemoration | of | The Living and Dead Soldiers | of Harvard University, | July 21, 1865. | By James Russell Lowell. | [device] | Cambridge: | Privately Printed. | 1865.

8vo. Collation: Title, limit notice and imprint, Note, Dedication of the poem, Dedication of this edition, and quotations, pp. [1–8]; text, pp. [9]–25. Size of leaf, untrimmed, 9⅝ by 6¹⁵⁄₁₆ inches.

Issued in gray boards, with paper label on front cover, "Commemoration | Ode."

Fifty copies only were printed, all for presentation. The note on p. [3] is as follows:

"Note. A few passages which would have made the Poem too long in the reading are added in this printed copy."

On p. [4] is the Dedication of the poem, as follows:

ODE

RECITED AT THE

COMMEMORATION

OF

THE LIVING AND DEAD SOLDIERS OF HARVARD UNIVERSITY,

July 21, 1865.

BY JAMES RUSSELL LOWELL.

CAMBRIDGE:

PRIVATELY PRINTED.

1865.

[SIZE OF ORIGINAL]

[72]

"To the ever sweet and shining memory of the Ninety-Three Sons of Harvard College Who have died for their Country in the War of Nationality, This Poem is Dedicated."

And the special Dedication of this edition, on p. [7], reads:

"This edition of my Commemoration Ode, printed for friends, is inscribed to those of my own kin who have fallen, not as singling them out for selfish praise, but because they were chiefly in my heart as I wrote. William Lowell Putnam. James Jackson Lowell. Charles Russell Lowell. Warren Dutton Lowell. Francis Dutton Lowell. Stephen George Perkins. Robert Gould Shaw. Cabot Russell."

This magnificent Ode was read by its author at Harvard's memorial celebration on July 21, 1865. Two days before, Lowell had told Prof. Child that he could write nothing—that he was "dull as a door-mat." But the next day inspiration came and the poem, as delivered, was written out in one night between ten o'clock and four in the morning. The sixth stanza, a powerful eulogium of Lincoln, was not in the poem as read, but was added a few days later.

The book was, no doubt, put in type and printed at once, as the inscriptions in several copies are dated September 3, 1865.

Two years later the poem was reprinted in the "Harvard Memorial Biographies," edited by Thomas Wentworth Higginson, filling pp. ix–xix of the preliminary pages of the first volume. Higginson evidently criticized the versification, and Lowell replied at length, suggesting changes, in a letter dated March 28, 1867, printed on pp. 379–382 of Vol. I of "Letters," 1894. The original manuscript of this letter was acquired by Mr. Chamberlain. None of the corrections and additions were made in the Ode as printed in the "Memorial Biographies." Colonel Higginson afterwards wrote: "Apparently I begged off from them, or perhaps they were just too late. Some years afterwards Lowell wrote me a letter (now lost) saying that he had kept no copy, and wished to use them. Apparently they could not then be found. One of the emendations he seems to have remembered and used."

This single correction is the one to which Lowell referred, as follows, in his letter of March 28, 1867: "On looking farther, I find to my intense disgust a verse without a mate in the last stanza but one, and I must put in a patch. If I had only kept my manuscript! We must read,

"'And bid her navies, that so lately hurled
Their crashing battle, hold their thunders in.'"

1865

The | Biglow Papers. | By | James Russell Lowell. | Second Series. | Authorized People's Edition. | London: | Trübner & Co. 60, Paternoster Row. | 1865.

[73]

12mo. Collation: Title, p. [i]; blank, p. [ii]; Contents, p. [1]; blank, p. [2]; text, pp. [3]–141; blank, p. [142]. No imprints. Size of leaf, trimmed, 6½ by 4¹⁄₁₆ inches.

Issued in green or blue paper covers, p. [1] reading, "The | Second Series | of the | Biglow Papers | by | James Russell Lowell. | Authorized People's Edition. | London: | Trübner & Co., Paternoster Row. | 1865", enclosed in a single-rule frame. Above the rule at the top is "Price one shilling." Pp. 2 and 3 of cover are blank. P. 4 has an advertisement of the first series of the "Biglow Papers."

The book consists of signatures A, B, C, D, E, F, G, H, and I, each 8 ll. The signature marks have been again rearranged, the book now making nine signatures of eight leaves each.

One additional piece was added to this edition, filling pp. 134–141. This is "Mr. Hosea Biglow to the Editor of the Atlantic Monthly," which first appeared in the number of that magazine for April, 1865.

1865

Good Company | For every Day in the year. | [quotation, 2 lines] | [Publishers' device] | Boston: | Ticknor and Fields. | 1866.

12mo. Collation: Blank, p. [1]; publishers' list of books, p. [2]; title, copyright (dated 1865) and imprint, and Contents, pp. [i]–iv; text, pp. 1–326. Portraits, separately printed, facing title and pp. 16, 19, 86, 110, 118, 134, 152, 168, 236, 240, 251, 265, 277, 288, 305, 308. Size of leaf, trimmed, 7½ by 4⅞ inches.

Issued in stamped cloth, back lettered "Good | Company."

This volume contains "Dara. | By James Russell Lowell." Pp. 16–18. It had appeared earlier in *Graham's Magazine* for July, 1850. It was collected in "Under the Willows," 1868.

1866

(No. 310.) | New England Loyal Publication Society. | Office, No. 8 Studio Building, Boston. | [rule] | April

[74]

23, 1866. | [double rule] | [Text in three columns, beginning:] A Speech that Mr. Johnson might | make. | (From an article entitled "The President on the Stump," in | the April number of the North American Review.)

Folio. A single sheet, printed on one side only. Size of type-page, 18 by 8$^{11}\!/_{16}$ inches.

The article in the *North American Review* for April, 1866, "The President on the Stump," was by James Russell Lowell. The extract here printed fills all of the first column of the sheet and eight lines at the top of the second column.

1866

A Christmas Carol. | (Written for the Children's Festival at the Church of Disciples, 1866.) | By James Russell Lowell. | (Not Published.) [Boston, 1866.]

8vo. A single sheet, printed on one side only, the above as a heading. The poem contains seven stanzas of four lines each. A "Christmas Hymn," two five-line stanzas, is appended. Size of type-page, 7 by 6⅜ inches.

This poem was collected in the "Heartsease and Rue" volume in 1888. The only copy of the broadside which I can trace is in the Aldis collection in Yale University Library.

The compilation "Poetry Lyrical, Narrative, and Satirical of the Civil War Selected and Edited by Richard Grant White.", New York, 1866, contains, on pp. 49–51, "Jonathan to John. | A Yankee Idyl. | By James Russell Lowell." This was first printed in the *Atlantic Monthly,* and reprinted in "Biglow Papers," Second Series, London, 1864.

1866

Melibœus-Hipponax. | [rule] | The | Biglow Papers. | Second Series. | [quotation, 13 lines] | [Publishers' device] | Boston: | Ticknor and Fields. | 1867.

A CHRISTMAS CAROL.

(Written for the Children's Festival at the Church of Disciples, 1866.)

By JAMES RUSSELL LOWELL.

[Not Published.]

1

"What means this glory round our feet,"
  The Magi mused, "more bright than morn?" } *First Chorus.*
And voices chanted clear and sweet,
  "To-day the Prince of Peace is born!" [*One voice.*]

2

"What means that star," the Shepherds said,
  "That brightens through the rocky glen?" } *Second Chorus.*
And angels, answering overhead,
  Sang, "Peace on earth, good-will to men!" [*One voice.*]

3

'T is eighteen hundred years and more
Since those sweet oracles were dumb;
We wait for Him like them of yore;
Alas, He seems so slow to come!

4

But it was said in words of gold,
  No time or sorrow e'er shall dim,
That little children might be bold,
  In perfect trust to come to Him.

5

All round about our feet shall shine
  A light like that the wise men saw,
If we our loving wills incline
  To that sweet Life which is the Law.

6

So shall we learn to understand
  The simple faith of shepherds then,
And kindly clasping hand in hand,
  Sing "Peace on earth, good-will to men!"

7

For they who to their childhood cling
And keep their natures fresh as morn,
Once more shall hear the angels sing,
"TO-DAY THE PRINCE OF PEACE IS BORN." [*Sung by one voice, repeated by whole Chorus.*]

CHRISTMAS HYMN.

1

Silent Night! Peaceful Night!
All things sleep — Shepherds keep
Watch on Bethlehem's holy hill;
And unseen, while all is still,
Angels watch above.

2

Light around! Joyful sound!
Angel voices fill the air,
"Glory be to God in Heaven,
Peace on Earth to you is given
From this Christmas morn."

[REDUCED IN SIZE]

12mo. Collation: Half-title, title, copyright (dated 1866) and imprint, pp. [1–4]; Dedication, quotations, Contents, and Introduction, pp. [i]–lxxx; text and Index, pp. 1–258. Size of leaf, trimmed, 7⅛ by 4½ inches.

Issued in cloth, back lettered "The | Biglow | Papers | Lowell | ** ".

Twelve copies were printed on large paper, size a small quarto, with the words "Biglow Papers" and "Boston" printed in red.

Of the eleven chapters which make up this volume, all but No. VIII, "Ketelopotomachia," and No. IX, called in the Contents "Table-Talk," had already been printed in the *Atlantic Monthly*, the last, No. XI, appearing in the number for March, 1866. And, as already noted, all but Nos. VIII, IX, and XI had been reprinted in book-form in London by Trübner & Co.

The volume was probably published about November 1, 1866, as the copy given by Lowell to John Bartlett contains an inscription dated "5th Nov. 1866." This copy contains several corrections in manuscript by Lowell in the Introduction. With two exceptions, the changes indicated were made in later editions.

It seems probable that the large-paper copies were printed off from the stereotype plates early in 1867. Only three of the twelve copies can now be traced. One, given to Longfellow and now in Harvard University Library, contains an inscription, "H. W. Longfellow | with the affectionate regards | of J. R. L. | 25th May 1867." It has on verso of title-page, in Lowell's autograph, "Twelve copies printed on large paper. J. R. L. No. 3."

The copy given to Charles Eliot Norton (also in the Harvard Library) has an inscription, "Christmas 1867," but is unnumbered. The third, in the library of the late Thomas Bailey Aldrich, "has several marginal notes by the author." Lowell sent it to Aldrich on December 23, 1868, with the letter printed on pp. 126–127 of Scudder's "James Russell Lowell A Biography." As the name of the book is not mentioned in the letter, Mr. Scudder may be excused his error of supposing it to have been a copy of the "Commemoration Ode." Under date of August 29, 1902, Mr. Aldrich wrote:

"Mr. Scudder made a mistake concerning the 'Commemoration Ode.' What Mr. Lowell gave me was a copy of 'The Biglow Papers'—one of a privately printed edition of 12 copies. The volume is a small quarto bound in blue cloth, and has several marginal notes by the author, making this copy unique.

"Mr. Lowell in his letter to me (page 126 Vol. II of Scudder's biography) does not name the book he sends. I believe that only two copies of this edition of 'Biglow Papers' are known. The other ten copies were stolen from an express cart, on its way from the University Press to Lowell's house. So far as I know, these volumes have not turned up."

"The Atlantic Almanac" for 1868 contains, on p. 37, "A June Day." This is an extract from "The Vision of Sir Launfal."

1868

Under the Willows | and | Other Poems. | By | James Russell Lowell. | Boston: | Fields, Osgood, & Co., | Successors to Ticknor and Fields. | 1869.

16mo.   Collation: Title, copyright (dated 1868) and imprint, Dedication, Note, and Contents, pp. [i]–viii; text, pp. [9]–286; slip of Erratum referring to p. 224 at end.   Size of leaf, trimmed, 6⅞ by 4⅝ inches.

Issued in cloth, back lettered "Under | The Willows | Lowell | Fields, Osgood & Co."

In the second issue the error indicated on the erratum slip, which reads in full: "Erratum. | Page 224, 2d stanza, 3d line, *for* Thy *read* Its.", was corrected.

Up to the issue of this volume in the fall of 1868, no new collection of Lowell's poems had appeared since that of 1849.   Besides poems which had already appeared in periodicals or annuals, some pieces written years before were touched up and utilized.   It was the author's intention at first to call the volume "A June Idyl and Other Poems," but James T. Fields, the publisher, told him that the title of Whittier's new volume was to be "A Summer Idyl," and so a change was made.   As a matter of fact, however, the title of Whittier's collection, when published, was "Among the Hills, and Other Poems."

The copy given to John Bartlett has an inscription dated "20th Nov'r., 1868", and the copy given to E. P. Whipple has a similar inscription dated "21st Nov'r, 1868."

The following interesting letter, relating to royalties on "Under the Willows," is worth printing:

"ELMWOOD, 7th May, 1869.

"DEAR SIR, This is to acknowledge the receipt from F. O. & Co. of a check for $416.75 (I wish it were for more!) & to say that I remain accessible, by mail or otherwise, to any further overtures you may please to make in the same kind.   Pray do not suspect me of insincerity if I add that you may print as many editions as you like on the same terms.   The dolts, it appears, begin to value my goods now that they have got an English ticket on 'em.   As their moral tendency (I mean the goods, not the dolts) is irreproachable I beg you to remember that 'be fruitful & multiply' was addressed to unfallen man.   Therefore exhaust the *plus* side of mathematics on my works—square 'em, cube 'em, & you will have the blessing of

"Yours very truly

"J. R. LOWELL."

1868

The | Atlantic Almanac | 1869 | Edited by Donald G. Mitchell. | [ornament] | Contents. | The entire Contents of the present number are original, both the Literary and Artistic Departments | having been prepared expressly for the Atlantic Almanac. | [31 lines] | Boston: | Ticknor and Fields, | Office of the Atlantic Monthly. | (Entered according to Act of Congress in the year 1868, by Ticknor and Fields, in the Clerk's Office of the District Court of the District of Massachusetts.)

Large 8vo. Collation: title and text, pp. [1]–66; advertisements, pp. [67]–80. Plates, separately printed, facing pp. 4, 16, 25, and 40. Size of leaf, untrimmed, 10⅛ by 8 inches.

Issued in lithographed paper covers, printed in colors, p. [1] reading, "The | Atlantic | Almanac | 1869 | Published at the office of the Atlantic Monthly. | Boston: Ticknor and Fields." Advertisements on pp. 2, 3, and 4 of cover.

On pp. 32, 33, 35, 36, and 37 is "My Garden Acquaintance. | By James Russell Lowell." This was collected in "My Study Windows," 1871. Pp. 34 and 38 contain the Calendar for September and October.

The pamphlet "Sixty-Third Anniversary Celebration of the New England Society in the City of New York at Delmonico's Dec. 22, 1868." contains, on p. 63, a letter from Lowell, dated "Cambridge, Dec. 17, 1868."

The collected edition of "Poems" published in 1869 contains this dedication: "To George William Curtis This first complete edition of my Poems is affectionately inscribed." The collection, apparently, contains nothing new.

1869

The | Atlantic Almanac | 1870 | With Illustrations by | Darley, Gilbert, Eytinge, Brown, Fenn, DuMaurier,

Homer, Fredericks, Hennessy, | Hoppin, Perkins and others. | [rule] | Table of Contents. | [25 lines] | Boston: | Fields, Osgood, & Co., | Office of the Atlantic Monthly. | (Entered according to Act of Congress, in the year 1869, by Fields, Osgood & Co., in the Clerk's Office of the District Court of the District of Massachusetts.)

Large 8vo. Collation: title and text, pp. [1]–64; advertisements, pp. 65–72. Plates separately printed, facing title and pp. 17 and 49. Size of leaf, trimmed, 10½ by 8 inches.

Issued in lithographed paper covers, printed in colors, p. [1] reading, "The | Atlantic | Almanac | 1870 | Published at the Office of the Atlantic Monthly. | Boston: Fields, Osgood & Co." Advertisements on pp. 2, 3, and 4 of cover.

Contains on pp. 39–41, 43–45, and 47, "A Good Word for Winter. | By James Russell Lowell." Pp. 42 and 46 contain the Calendar for November and December.

A pamphlet printed as an advertisement of "George W. Minns' Scientific, Classical and Commercial School for Boys," Boston, 1869, contains, on p. 6, a short testimonial letter from J. R. Lowell.

1870

Among my Books. | By | James Russell Lowell, A.M., | Professor of Belles-Lettres in Harvard College. | [Publishers' device] | Boston: | Fields, Osgood, & Co. | 1870.

12mo. Collation: Blank, p. [1]; list of Lowell's writings, p. [2]; title, copyright (dated 1870) and imprint, Dedication, and Contents, pp. [i–v]; text, pp. 1–380. Size of leaf, trimmed, 7¼ by 4¾ inches.

Issued in cloth, back lettered "Among | My Books | Lowell".

This, Lowell's second volume of prose essays, was published in February, 1870. The six essays had all appeared earlier in the columns of the *North American Review.* On July 6, 1869, Lowell wrote: "I have not forgotten the volume of Essays. They come into my Budget for the year '69. I shall have them ready in a few weeks from now. I have been adding & annotating more or less all summer. I want them to be as good as I can make them. I propose to include only the critical ones, & only the best of those. Two hundred & fifty or three hundred pages, I suppose, will be as much as you want—so that six essays at most will fill up."

1870

The Cathedral. | By | James Russell Lowell. | [vignette] | Boston: | Fields, Osgood, & Co. | 1870.

12mo. Collation: Blank, p. [1]; list of Lowell's writings, p. [2]; half-title, quotation, title, copyright (dated 1869) and imprint, and Dedication, pp. [i–v]; text, pp. 7–[53]. Size of leaf, trimmed, 6⅞ by 4⅝ inches.

Issued in stamped cloth, back lettered lengthwise "The Cathedral".

This poem, which was first called "A Day at Chartres," was written during the summer of 1869. In a letter to Charles Eliot Norton, Lowell says: "I wrote in pencil, then copied it out in ink, and worked over it as I never worked over anything before. I may fairly say there is not a word in it over which I have not thought, nor an objection which I did not foresee and maturely consider. Well, in my second copy I made many changes, as I thought for the better, and then put it away in my desk to cool for three weeks or so. When I came to print it, I put back, I believe, *every one* of the original readings which I had changed."

The poem was first printed in the *Atlantic Monthly* for January, 1870, which was published early in December, 1869. Later in the month this volume appeared. From another letter, also written to Norton, we learn that it was an earlier text which had appeared in the magazine. In that letter, dated December 10, 1869, he says: "Those who have seen it think well of it. I shall contrive to send it you, and beg you not to read it in the *Atlantic*—for I have restored to it (they are printing it separately) some omitted passages, besides correcting a phrase here and there whose faultiness the stronger light of print revealed to me."

1870

Tributes   to   the Memory of | Hon. John Pendleton Kennedy. | [Boston, 1870.]

8vo. Collation: No title-page, above at top of p. [1]; text, pp. [1]–16. Size of leaf, trimmed, 9¼ by 5⅞ inches.

Issued in paper cover, p. [1] with legend, "Tributes to the Memory of | Hon. John Pendleton Kennedy. | Reprinted from the Proceedings of the Massachusetts Historical Society." Other cover pages blank.

Lowell's remarks are found on pp. 12–14, beginning: "Professor James Russell Lowell then said:—", etc.

While these "Tributes" were actually first printed in the Proceedings of the Society, this separate form is the more desirable. They first appeared in the pamphlet, without title, but with legend on the cover: "VII. | Proceedings | of the | Massachusetts Historical Society, | for | June, July, August, and September, 1870." The book is paged 321–384, Lowell's remarks being on pp. 365–367.

1870

The | Poets and Poetry | of | Europe. | with | Introductions and Biographical Notices. | By | Henry Wadsworth Longfellow. | A New Edition, Revised and Enlarged. | [quotation, 3 lines] | Philadelphia: | Porter and Coates, 822 Chestnut Street. | 1871.

8vo. Collation: Half-title, title, copyright (dated 1870) and imprint, Preface, Contents, Contents of the Supplement, Index of Authors, Index of Authors—Supplement, Translators, and Sources, Translators and Sources—Supplement, pp. [i–xxvii]; text, pp. 1–776; text of Supplement, pp. [778]–916. Frontispiece (portrait of Goethe) and engraved title, separately printed. Size of leaf, trimmed, 9⅝ by 6¹³⁄₁₆ inches.

Issued in stamped cloth, back lettered "Poets & Poetry | of | Europe | Henry W. Longfellow | Porter & Coates."

This new edition was printed from the stereotyped plates used for the 1845 edition, but with a Supplement and additional preliminary pages. It was published in December, 1870.

The Supplement contains one poem, "To Madame du Chatelet," translated from Voltaire by Lowell, p. 841. Lowell's name does not appear with the poem, but in the "Contents," p. xvii, his name is given as translator. The list of "Translators and Sources," p. xxvii, states that the contribution was printed from manuscript, and it was probably translated at Longfellow's request. In the Morgan library there is a manuscript of this poem in Lowell's autograph, signed "J. R. Lowell" and dated "14th Feby, 1871." On the same sheet is the following letter:

"MY DEAR MISS ALGER

"I send you a translation from a little poem of Voltaire. I have hardly done justice (not to say shown mercy) to the charm of the original. But it will serve the purpose for which you want it, I hope.

"Very truly yours.

"J. R. LOWELL"

As the poem was printed in Longfellow's volume, published in December, 1870, this manuscript sent to Miss Alger cannot be the original. The poem has never been reprinted in any collected edition of Lowell's works.

1871

My Study Windows. | By | James Russell Lowell, A.M., | Professor of Belles-Lettres in Harvard College. | [Publishers' device] | Boston: | James R. Osgood and Company, | Late Ticknor & Fields, and Fields, Osgood, & Co. | 1871.

12mo. Collation: Blank, p. [1]; list of Lowell's writings, p. [2]; title, copyright (dated 1871) and imprint, Prefatory Note, Dedication, and Contents, pp. [i–v]; text, pp. 1–433. Size of leaf, trimmed, 7¾₁₆ by 4⅞ inches.

Issued in cloth, back lettered "My Study | Windows | Lowell".

Copies of the first binding have the monogram of Fields, Osgood & Co. stamped at the bottom on the back, while later bindings have the monogram of James R. Osgood & Co. The monogram on the title-page of all copies seems to be that of James R. Osgood & Co., but Mr. Chamberlain made a memorandum to look for copies without monogram on title, or with that of Fields, Osgood & Co.

The Dedication is dated "Christmas 1870", and the book was published in January, 1871. The copies presented to E. P. Whipple and to John Bartlett contain each an inscription dated January 20, 1871. On December 26, 1870, Lowell wrote to his publishers:

"I send you a prefatory note, & a dedication. I would rather the Pope should not go in, but you shall have your own way about it. I could not give it my last hand. If the book could wait till the middle of February, I might improve it. But you know best about that."

The "Pope" did go in, and is the last essay in the volume.

On July 31, 1871, he was "waiting for a new edition, in which the misprints are corrected", before sending a copy of the book to Norton.

The Preface says that "the papers here gathered have been written at intervals during the last fifteen years." All had appeared in magazines except "My Garden Acquaintance" and "A Good Word for Winter," which, as already noted, appeared in "The Atlantic Almanac" for 1869 and 1870.

The pamphlet "Reception tendered by the members of the Union League of Philadelphia to George H. Boker, Minister of the United States to Turkey. Friday Evening, December 22, 1871.", Philadelphia, 1872, contains, on p. 61, a letter from James Russell Lowell, six lines, dated "Elmwood, 18th Dec. 1871," regretting his inability to be present.

1872

His Imperial Highness | The Grand Duke Alexis | in the | United States of America | During the Winter of 1871–72 | [quotation, 2 lines] | For Private Distribution | Cambridge | Printed at the Riverside Press | 1872

8vo. Collation: Title and note, pp. [i–iii]; text and Index, pp. [1–223]. With photographic frontispiece. Size of leaf, trimmed, 10 by 6¾ inches.

Issued in full leather, back lettered "The | Grand Duke | Alexis | in the | United States".

It is said that only fifty copies were printed at the expense of G. V. Fox, who had been the recipient of courtesies at the Court of Russia, and who took this method of showing his appreciation of the treatment accorded him there. The volume contains, on pp. 102–104, a speech by Lowell, "Mr. Lowell said,—" which has never been reprinted.

One copy which I have seen has the inscription: "Presented to the Library | of the | M. M. Association | Lowell Oct. 2, 1872. | G. V. Fox."

I have seen another copy with slightly different title. The two lines of quotation are higher on the page, and the line "For Private Distribution" is lowered. Between the two are two new lines " | By | William W. Tucker |." This copy is without the photographic frontispiece, which it seems never to have had. It is bound in half morocco, cloth sides, marbled edges, back lettered " | Grand | Duke | Alexis | ". Otherwise the two are identical.

The "Catalogue of the School of Modern Languages.", Cambridge, 1872, contains, among other testimonials, a letter from Lowell, dated "Cambridge, May 24, 1872." It is found on p. 24.

1874

Jeffries Wyman. | Memorial Meeting | of the | Boston Society of Natural History | October 7, 1874. [Boston, 1874.]

8vo. Collation: Title, Contents, and text, pp. [1]–[39]. Size of leaf, untrimmed, 9⅞ by 6⅛ inches.

Issued in paper cover, p. 1 printed from the types of the title-page. Other cover-pages blank.

On p. [3] is "Jeffries Wyman. | Died 4th September, 1874.", signed "J. R. L." These verses were first printed in the *Nation* of October 8, 1874. They were collected in "Heartsease and Rue," 1888.

A pamphlet, pp. 1–16, being an advertisement of "The Complete Works of Charles Sumner," contains, on p. 7, a letter "From James Russell Lowell," beginning: "I am glad to hear that you have undertaken an edition of Mr. Sumner's collected works," etc. The only copy I have seen was bound at the end of a copy of "Prophetic Voices Concerning America. A Monograph. By Charles Sumner." Boston, 1874.

A short letter from Lowell, regretting his inability to attend a dinner given by the New England Society in New York, is printed on p. 90 of an octavo pamphlet having the title: "Sixty-Ninth Anniversary Celebration of the New England Society in the City of New York at Delmonico's Dec. 22, 1874."

1875

Proceedings | at the | Centennial Celebration | of | Concord Fight | April 19, 1875. | [vignette] | Concord, Mass. | Published by the Town. | 1876.

Large 8vo. Collation: Half-title, title, Preface, and Contents, pp. [1–7]; half-title, text, etc., pp. [9–176]. Portraits, separately printed, facing pp. [8] and [18], a vignette facing p. 74, and a facsimile, a folded sheet, facing p. [164]. Size of leaf, trimmed, 10⅜ by 6¾ inches.

Issued in cloth, back lettered "Centennial | of | Concord | Fight". Also in paper cover, p. [1], "1775. | Concord Fight. | 1875." Other cover-pages blank.

This volume contains: "Mr. Lowell then read the following:— | Ode. | I. | Who cometh over the hills,". Pp. 82–88.

This Ode appeared in the *Atlantic Monthly* for June, 1875. It was collected in the volume "Three Memorial Poems" the next year.

1875

Cambridge in the "Centennial." | [ornament] | Proceedings, | July 3, 1875, | in celebration of the | Centennial Anniversary | of | Washington's taking command | of the | Continental army, | On Cambridge Common. | [coat of arms] | Cambridge: | Printed by order of the City Council. | M DCCC LXXV.

Large 8vo. Collation: Title, Order of Council and imprint, and Contents, pp. [1]–4; text, pp. [5–127]; Frontispiece, the Washington Elm, separately printed, facing title, and plate, Soldiers' Monument, facing p. 117. Size of leaf, trimmed, 9½ by 6⅜ inches.

Issued in gray paper cover, p. [1] printed from the types of the title surrounded by a border. Also issued in cloth, back lettered "Cambridge | July 3rd | 1775 | 1875".

This volume contains "Poem, | By | James Russell Lowell." Pp. [27]–38. At the end is the following note:

"NOTE:—The Poem by Prof. Lowell (as well as that by Dr. Holmes) is here printed by permission of H. O. Houghton & Co., publishers of the *Atlantic Monthly,* with alterations and additional lines."

This poem, when it appeared in the *Atlantic Monthly,* had the title "Under the Great Elm," altered in the current editions to "Under the Old Elm." It was collected the next year in the volume "Three Memorial Poems."

The present volume also contains, on p. 87, " 'The Poet of the Day'. Response by Prof. James Russell Lowell, of Cambridge, the Poet of the Day." Twelve lines, in prose.

1875

The Harvard Book. | A Series of | Historical, Biograph-
ical, | and Descriptive | Sketches. | By | Various
Authors. | Illustrated with Views and Portraits. | Col-
lected and published | By | F. O. Vaille and H. A.
Clark, | Class of 1874. | Vol. I. | [Vol. II.] | Cam-
bridge: | Welch, Bigelow, and Company, | University
Press. | 1875.

2 vols., 4to. Collation: Vol. I: Half-title, title, copyright (dated
1875), Dedication, Preface, Contents, and Illustrations, pp. [i–
xx]; half-title and text, pp. [21–347]. With plates, separately
printed, as enumerated in the list on pp. [xvii–xx]. Vol. II:
Half-title, title, copyright, Contents, and Illustrations, pp. [i]–
xiv; text, pp. [15]–447. Plates, separately printed, as enumerated in the list on p. xiv. Size of leaf, trimmed, 13½ by 10¾
inches.

Pp. [157]–172 contain "Class Day," by James Russell Lowell. This has,
apparently, never been reprinted.

1875

Sheets for the Cradle | [double rule] | "Ipsa tibi blan-
dos fundent cunabula flores." | [double rule] | Vol. I.
—No. 1. Boston, December 6, 1875. Price 15
Cents.

4to. Consists of six numbers, the above being the heading of
No. 1. Nos. 2–6 are dated December 7, 8, 9, 10, and 11. Each
number consists of eight pages, numbered [1]–8. Size of leaf,
trimmed, 11½ by 9 inches.

This little paper, edited by Susan Hale, was published "daily at 5 P.M."
for "The Grand Fair in Aid of the Massachusetts Infant Asylum." No. 5

contains, on p. [1], "An Anecdote of Walter Savage Landor. | James Russell Lowell." This has never been collected.

An advertising pamphlet published by the *Nation,* with the title, "Worth Reading. An Ideal Reformer. From 'The Nation.' New York, 1875," contains two pieces in verse by Lowell. "What Rabbi Jehosha Said," on p. [10], had already been collected in "Under the Willows" in 1868. "Jeffries Wyman | Died 4th September, 1874" had been printed in the "Memorial" in 1874. It was collected by Lowell in "Heartsease and Rue."

1875

Laurel Leaves. | Original | Poems, Stories, and Essays, | By | Henry W. Longfellow, John G. Whittier, Oliver Wendell Holmes, William | Cullen Bryant, James Russell Lowell, | J. T. Trowbridge, E. P. Whipple, | T. W. Higginson, | Louisa M. Alcott, | Gail Hamilton, Harriet Prescott | Spofford, H.H., Louise Chandler Moulton, Nora Perry, Sarah | Helen Whitman, Margaret J. Preston, Bayard Taylor, R. H. | Stoddard, Alfred Tennyson, A. C. Swinburne, Charles Kings- | ley, Tom Taylor, Edward Eggleston, J. W. DeForrest, | George Cary Eggleston, William Ellery Channing, | J. Boyle O'Reilly, William Winter, Edward S. | Rand, Jr. William Mathews, A. Bronson Al- | cott, Charles Dudley Warner, John Paul, | William F. Gill, Frederic Viaux. | Illustrated. | Boston: | William F. Gill and Company, | 309 Washington Street. | [rule] | 1876.

8vo. Collation: Title, copyright (dated 1875) and imprint, pp. [i–ii]; half-title, Dedication, Facsimile, Preface, Contents, and List of Illustrations, pp. [iii]–xv; half-titles and text, pp. [17]–446. Size of leaf, trimmed, 8½ by 6⁹⁄₁₆ inches.

Issued in cloth, back lettered "Laurel | Leaves".

This volume contains two pieces by Lowell: (1) "Gloria Mundi. | By James Russell Lowell." P. 103. This has never been collected. (2) "To a Friend, | who gave me a Group of Weeds and | Grasses. | (After a drawing of Dürer.) J. R. Lowell." P. 302. This had appeared in *The Mercantile*, March 21, 1875. It was collected in "Heartsease and Rue," 1888.

"The Ark," edited by Susan Hale for a fair held by the Society for the Prevention of Cruelty to Animals, and of which eight numbers were published from February 22 to March 2, 1875, contains eight lines of verse by James Russell Lowell, beginning:

"The little bird sits at his door in the sun."

This is an extract from "The Vision of Sir Launfal," published in 1848.

1876

Among my Books. | Second Series. | By | James Russell Lowell, | Professor of Belles-Lettres in Harvard College. | [Publishers' device] | Boston: | James R. Osgood and Company, | Late Ticknor & Fields, and Fields, Osgood, & Co. | 1876.

12mo. Collation: Blank, p. [1]; list of Lowell's writings, p. [2]; title, copyright (dated 1875) and imprint, Dedication, and Contents, pp. [i–v]; text, pp. 1–327. Size of leaf, trimmed, 7¼ by 4⅞ inches.

Issued in cloth, back lettered "Among | My Books | Lowell".

In the earliest issue, apparently a few copies only, the copyright entry on reverse of title is dated 1875. The book was not published until January, 1876, and most copies have the copyright date corrected to 1876.

On July 4, 1875, Lowell wrote to James R. Osgood, his publisher:
"You will remember that I fixed 'after Commencement' as the date after which I should have enough collectedness of mind to go on with the volume. I shall take up my proofs again on Tuesday, and hurry as fast as conscience will allow."

The work was "broken off by an illness," and on November 20 he was still "fussing over the volume . . ." and "fussing, too, without much progress." On December 15 he wrote: "This is the first day I have had free of proof-sheets." On December 25 he wrote to a correspondent whose name Professor Norton does not give: "I had hoped before this to have sent you my new book, but it hung long on my hands and is not yet out."

On January 17, 1876, he wrote to the same correspondent: "I sent you day before yesterday [*i.e.* January 15] my new book, and that copy was the first I sent to any one." Nevertheless the copy presented by Lowell to Professor Norton has an inscription dated January 13.

Later, on May 15, Lowell wrote to Leslie Stephen:

"I have published another volume, and I ought long ago to have sent you a copy, but I took a disgust at it so soon as I saw it in print. I was really ill all the time it was going through the press, so that I sometimes could not even read a proof for weeks, and had to put in at random some things I would rather have left for a posthumous edition of my works (if I ever have one), when people read with kindlier eyes."

This volume includes five essays: "Dante," "Spenser," "Wordsworth," "Milton," and "Keats." Three of them had already appeared in the *North American Review,* the "Milton" in January, 1872, as a review of Masson's "Life of Milton"; the "Dante" in July, 1872, as a review of Miss Rossetti's "The Shadow of Dante"; and the "Spenser" in April, 1875. The "Keats" and "Wordsworth" are the introductions written for the works of these two poets in 1854, but both are in large part rewritten.

1876

Three Memorial Poems. | By | James Russell Lowell. | [quotation, 1 line] | Boston: | James R. Osgood and Company, | Late Ticknor & Fields, and Fields, Osgood, & Co. | 1877.

12mo. Collation: Blank, p. [1]; list of Lowell's writings, p. [2]; half-title, title, copyright (dated 1876) and imprint, Dedication, ornament, Poem, To the Readers, Contents, ornament, half-title, ornament, and text, pp. [1]–92. Size of leaf, trimmed, 6¾ by 5⅛ inches.

Issued in cloth, back lettered lengthwise "Three Memorial Poems Lowell".

The three poems which make up the volume are:
"Ode read at Concord, April 19, 1875."
"Under the Old Elm."
"An Ode for the Fourth of July, 1876."
The first two had been included in the volumes issued to commemorate the Battle of Concord, and Washington's taking command of the Army, as already noted. The Fourth of July Ode appeared in the *Atlantic*

Monthly for December, 1876, published, we may presume, almost simultaneously with this volume.

Besides these poems there is a preliminary sonnet, "If I let fall a word of bitter mirth," here first printed.

A privately printed pamphlet having the title: "Alpha Delta Phi Reunion Dinner In New York 1875 With a Register of Members in New York," New York, 1876, contains, on p. 16, a letter, six lines, dated "Elmwood, 17th, Nov. 1875" and signed "J. R. Lowell."

"Silhouettes and Songs," a volume of illustrations and selections published in Boston, in 1876, contains, as a selection for May, an extract from "The Biglow Papers," Second Series, beginning "Jes' so our Spring gits everythin' in tune."

1877

Old South Meeting-House. | Report | of a | Meeting of the inhabitants of Cambridge, | in | Memorial Hall, Harvard College, | January 18th, 1877. | [rule] | Addresses by | President Charles W. Eliot, | Prof. James Russell Lowell, | Rev. Alexander McKenzie, | Hon. Charles T. Russell, | Chief-Justice Charles L. Bradley, | Rev. George Z. Gray, | Rev. George W. Briggs. | [rule] | Boston: | Press of George H. Ellis. | 1877.

8vo. Collation: Title and text, pp. [1]–29. Size of leaf, trimmed, 9 by 5¾ inches.

Issued in gray paper cover, p. [1] printed from the types of the title-page, but within a double-rule frame. Other coverpages blank.

The "Address of James Russell Lowell." occupies pp. 6-10. It seems never to have been reprinted.

1877

Tribute | of the | Massachusetts Historical Society | To the Memory | of | Edmund Quincy | and | John

Lothrop Motley | [rule] | Boston | Massachusetts
Historical Society | 1877

8vo. Collation: Title, imprint, and text, pp. [1]–30. Size of
leaf, untrimmed, 9¾ by 6⅛ inches.

Issued in paper cover, p. 1 printed from the types of the title-
page, but within a double-rule frame.

Lowell's tribute to Quincy, headed: "Professor James Russell Lowell
then said:", is on pp. 9–11.
In the "Proceedings" of the Society for 1876 and 1877, Boston, 1878,
these "Remarks" occur on pp. 286, 287. The section containing pp. 249 to
404 of the volume was issued somewhat earlier than this separate. It is
in paper cover, with cover title: "III. | Proceedings | of the | Massa-
chusetts Historical Society. | March to December, 1877. | (Inclusive.)"

1877

Golden Songs of Great Poets. | [ornament] | Regia,
Crede mihi, res est. | [ornament] | Illustrated by |
Darley, Moran, Hart, Fredericks, Smillie, and Mc-
Entee. | [ornament] | New York: | Sarah H. Leggett,
| No. 1184 Broadway. | 1877.

8vo. Collation: Title, copyright (dated 1877), Contents, blank
leaf, and engraved title, pp. [i–xi]; half-title and text, 41 leaves
printed on recto only. Size of leaf, trimmed, 8⅞ by 6¾ inches.

Issued in stamped cloth, back lettered lengthwise "Golden
Songs of Great Poets." Front cover with facsimile signatures,
in gilt, of Bryant, Longfellow, Whittier, Lowell, Taylor, and
Holmes.

"The Fire-Fly: A Parable," by Lowell, occupies three leaves. This
was first collected in "Heartsease and Rue," 1888.

1877

Papers | Relating to the | Foreign Relations | of | The
United States. | Transmitted to Congress, | With the

Annual Message of the President, | December 3, 1877. | Preceded by a | List of Papers and followed by an Index of | Persons and Subjects. | [rule] | Washington: | Government Printing Office. | 1877.

8vo. Collation: Title, Message, and List, pp. [i]–xlviii; text and Index, pp. 1–654. Size of leaf, trimmed, 9 by 5¾ inches.

Issued in cloth, back lettered "Message | And Documents | Dep't. State | 1878–79."

Mr. Lowell was appointed by President Hayes as United States Minister to Spain, and he arrived at Madrid on August 14, 1877. On the 18th of the same month he was presented at court and took up the duties of his office. This volume (and others to be described later) contains some of his letters, addressed to the Secretary of State and to others, on official business. Selections were republished in the volume "Impressions of Spain" and extracts are included in Scudder's Life of Lowell, but the mass of his correspondence is unpublished elsewhere.

Each of these volumes was also issued with a different title, "Index to the Executive Documents of the House of Representatives," etc., and with some additional matter. That form is a reissue, the imprint being always a year later.

The present volume includes a letter from Mr. Lowell to Secretary of State Evarts, dated "Madrid, October 12, 1877", together with four other documents by him, addressed to Mr. Silvela, Spanish Minister of State. These occupy pp. 521–525.

"The Life of Edgar Allan Poe" by William F. Gill, New York and Philadelphia, 1877, contains, on pp. 152–158, Lowell's article on Poe, extracted from *Graham's Magazine* for February, 1845, which had been reprinted earlier in Griswold's edition of Poe's works, 1850. The volume also contains, on p. 283, a letter (seven lines) from Lowell to Miss Sarah S. Rice, Corresponding Secretary of the Poe Monument Association, Baltimore.

The "Memorial of Fitz-Greene Halleck," New York, 1877, contains, on p. 40, a short letter from Lowell, dated "Elmwood, 7th May, 1877."

1878

No Name Series. | "Is the Gentleman anonymous? Is he a great unknown?" | Daniel Deronda. | [ornament] | A | Masque of Poets. | Including | Guy Ver-

·non, a Novelette in Verse. | Boston: | Roberts Brothers. | 1878.

16mo. Collation: Half-title, title, copyright (dated 1878), Contents, quotation, vignette, pp. [1–10]; text, pp. [11]–301; quotation, vignette, and quotation, p. [302]. Publishers' lists on lining papers, front and back. A slip, printed on colored paper, beginning, "Publishers' Notice. | Editors and all others reprinting single poems, etc.", is inserted before the title-page. Size of leaf, trimmed, 6⁹⁄₁₆ by 4⅜ inches.

Issued in cloth, back lettered "A | Masque | of Poets | No Name Series | Roberts | Brothers | Boston".

This volume contains two short poems by Lowell: (1) "My Heart, I cannot still it," p. 142. Collected in "Heartsease and Rue," 1888, with the title "Auspex." (2) "Red Tape," p. 153. This was also included in the "Heartsease and Rue" volume, but with title altered to "The Brakes."

1878

Papers | Relating to the | Foreign Relations | of | The United States, | Transmitted to Congress, | With the Annual Message of the President, | December 2, 1878. | Preceded by a | List of Papers and followed by an Index of | Persons and Subjects. | [rule] | Washington: | Government Printing Office. | 1878.

8vo. Collation: Title, Message, and List, pp. [i]–xlviii; text and Index, pp. [1]–976. Size of leaf, trimmed, 9 by 5¾ inches.

Issued in cloth, back lettered "Message | and | Documents | Dep't. State | 1878–'79".

This volume includes nineteen letters from Lowell, thirteen having been addressed to Secretary of State Evarts, and six to Mr. Silvela, the Spanish Minister of State. They occupy, with other correspondence, pp. 764–804. The selections printed by Mr. Gilder are taken from this volume and the next.

The "Diary of Samuel Sewall," forming Volumes V, VI, and VII of the Fifth Series of the Collections of the Massachusetts Historical Society, was prepared for the press by a Committee of Publications consisting of George E. Ellis, William H. Whitmore, Henry Warren Torrey, and James Russell Lowell. The first volume appeared in 1878, the second in 1879, and the third in 1882. Lowell, probably, had very little to do with it, and no collector would care to include à set among his first editions of Lowell's works.

Lowell's poem "The Rose," published separately, with illustrations, in 1878, is one of his earliest pieces, having been printed first in *The Pioneer* in 1843 and collected in "Poems," 1844.

1879

Papers | Relating to the | Foreign Relations | of | The United States, | Transmitted to Congress, | With the Annual Message of the President, | December 1, 1879. | Preceded by a | List of Papers and followed by an Index of | Persons and Subjects. | [rule] | Washington: | Government Printing Office. | 1879.

8vo. Collation: Title, Message, and List, pp. [i]–lxxiv; text and Index, pp. [1]–1093. Size of leaf, trimmed, 9 by 5¾ inches.
    Issued in cloth, back lettered "Message | and | Documents. | Dep't State. | 1879."

Twelve letters from Lowell are included in this volume, nine addressed to Secretary of State Evarts, and three to the Spanish Minister of State, Mr. Silvela, and his successor in office, the Duke of Tetuan. They occupy, with related correspondence, pp. 935–955. The first of the series of letters to Evarts, dated October 29, 1878, had already been printed in the preceding volume of "Papers."

In 1879 Allan Thorndike Rice reprinted a number of contributions to the *North American Review* in a volume with the title, "Essays from the North American Review." Lowell's "Shakespeare Once More," which had appeared in the magazine for April, 1868, occupies pp. 377–432. It had, however, already appeared in "Among My Books," published in 1870.

1880

Spare Minute Series. | True Manliness. | From the Writings of Thomas Hughes. | Selected by | E. E.

Brown. | With an Introduction by | James Russell Lowell. | Boston: | D. Lothrop and Co., | Franklin Street, Corner of Hawley.

8vo. Collation: Title, copyright (dated 1880), Biographical Sketch, "Thomas Hughes", pp. [iii]–xxii; text, pp. 13–300; Index, pp. ccci, cccii. Publishers' list bound in at end, pp. [1–10]. Size of leaf, trimmed, 7¼₆ by 4¹¹⁄₁₆ inches.

Issued in cloth, back lettered "True | Manliness | Thomas Hughes | Introduction By | J. R. Lowell | Boston | D. Lothrop & Co."

There is a "Preliminary Note", signed at end "J. R. L.," on pp. v, vi. Judge Hughes was one of Lowell's dearest friends in England.

1880

Papers | Relating to the | Foreign Relations | of | The United States, | Transmitted to Congress, | With the Annual Message of the President, | December 6, 1880. | Preceded by a | List of Papers and followed by an Index of | Persons and Subjects. | [rule] | Washington: | Government Printing Office. | 1880.

8vo. Collation: Title, Message, and List, pp. [i]–lxxxvii; text and Index, pp. [1]–1091. Size of leaf, trimmed, 9 by 5¾ inches.

Issued in cloth, back lettered "Message | and | Documents | Dep't State | 1880–'81".

Two letters from Lowell to Secretary of State Evarts, and two others to the Spanish Minister of State, are printed on pp. 887–890. Lowell was, during the year, transferred to the Court of St. James, arriving in London on March 7, 1880. Four letters from Lowell to Evarts, two to Lord Granville, and one to Lieutenant Greely are printed on pp. 479–484; also a short letter to Secretary Evarts on p. 588.

1881

Death of President Garfield | Meeting of Americans in London | At Exeter Hall 24 September 1881 | To which is added by permission | The Address of | His Grace the Archbishop of Canterbury | Delivered at the church of | St. Martin's-in-the-Fields | 26 September 1881 | [ornament] | London: Benjamin Franklin Stevens | 4 Trafalgar Square Charing Cross | 1881

8vo. Collation: Half-title, title, Preface, and text, pp. [1]–60. Imprint at bottom of p. 60. Photograph of Garfield facing title. Size of leaf, untrimmed, 8¼ by 6 inches.

Issued in white cloth, front cover printed from the types of the half-title, "In Memoriam | James Abram Garfield | Born 19 November 1831 | Died 19 September 1881".

Another edition, printed on inferior paper, was issued in blue paper covers, with trimmed edges. Five copies were printed on vellum, apparently at a later date.

The Preface, pp. 5–8, is by Lowell; also the Address, pp. 11–21.

In a presentation copy from Lowell to Benjamin H. Ticknor there is a manuscript correction in line 8, p. 5, "sincere" being changed to "spontaneous". It was this which led Mr. Chamberlain to suppose that the book was compiled by Lowell and that he wrote the Preface. He sought for confirmation of this from Mr. Charles Eliot Norton, who replied, in a letter dated December 5, 1902:

"In looking at my copy of the Garfield Memorial volume, my impression is confirmed that Mr. Lowell did not write the Preface. If I remember correctly, he told me that the volume was got up by Mr. B. F. Stevens, and I am inclined to believe that Mr. Stevens was the author of the Preface."

Nevertheless Mr. Norton was mistaken, for I have seen two pages of the "Preface" in Lowell's autograph. *With it was one of the five copies of the book printed on vellum, containing this inscription:

"To | Mr. B. F. Stevens, | with the sincere regards | of | J. R. Lowell. | (Five copies printed on vellum at the suggestion | & under the superintendence of Mr. Stevens.) No. 2."

This copy of the book was accompanied by the following letter, dated "10th September, 1883":

"DEAR MR. STEVENS,

"One of the Copies belongs naturally to you & if it did n't I should prefer to give it that destination. So pray accept it.

"I enclose my check to your order for £24-7-6 to pay charges of printing.

"Faithfully yours

"J. R. LOWELL."

This manuscript, book, and letter are owned by Mr. Henry W. Thompson (long an associate of Mr. Stevens), to whom they were presented by Mrs. Stevens. What disposition Mr. Lowell made of the four other copies on vellum I have been unable to trace.

Lowell's address was reprinted in "Democracy and Other Addresses," 1884.

In the printed "Exercises in celebrating the Two Hundred and Fiftieth Anniversary of the Settlement of Cambridge, Held December 28, 1880," Cambridge, 1881, a letter from Lowell, dated "Legation of the United States, London, Dec. 5, 1880," occupies p. 12.

1882

Sir Walter Raleigh | and | America. | [rule] | A Sermon | Preached at | St. Margaret's Church, Westminster, | on May 14, 1882, | By the Rev. Canon Farrar, D.D., F.R.S., | At the Unveiling of the | "Raleigh Window," | The Gift of American Citizens. | [rule] | Published by Request. | [rule] | London: | Printed at the "Anglo-American Times" Press, | 127, Strand, W C

8vo. Collation: No title-page, above is p. [1] of cover. Preface and text, pp. [1]–21. Plate, a photograph mounted on a sheet, separately printed, facing p. [1]. Size of leaf, trimmed, 9⅝ by 5⁹⁄₁₆ inches.

Issued in paper cover, p. [1] as above. Other cover-pages blank.

Lowell's lines written for the Raleigh window are printed on p. 7. The same four lines are printed below the photographic frontispiece. They were collected in "Heartsease and Rue."

1882

Papers | Relating to the | Foreign Relations | of | The United States, | Transmitted to Congress, | With the

Annual Message of the President, | December 5, 1881. | Preceded by a | List of Papers and followed by an Index of | Persons and Subjects. | [rule] | Washington: | Government Printing Office. | 1882.

8vo. Collation: Title, Message, and List, pp. [i]–xcii; text and Index, pp. [1]–1250. Size of leaf, trimmed, 9 by 5¾ inches.

Issued in cloth, back lettered "Message | and | Documents | Dep't State. | 1881–'82."

On pp. 492–560, interspersed with related correspondence, there are printed thirty-four letters and notes of James Russell Lowell. Three are addressed to William M. Evarts, Secretary of State; fourteen to his successor in office, James G. Blaine; eleven to Earl Granville; and six to other correspondents.

1883

Papers | Relating to the | Foreign Relations | of | The United States, | Transmitted to Congress, | With the Annual Message of the President, | December 4, 1882. | Preceded by a | List of Papers and followed by an Index of | Persons and Subjects. | [rule] | Washington: | Government Printing Office. | 1883.

8vo. Collation: Title, Message, and List, pp. [i]–liii; text and Index, pp. [1]–557. Size of leaf, trimmed, 9 by 5¾ inches.

Issued in cloth, back lettered "Message | and | Documents | Dep't State. | 1882–'83."

This volume includes, scattered through other correspondence between pp. 192 and 291, sixty-two letters by Lowell. Twenty-three were addressed to the Secretary of State, Frederick T. Frelinghuysen; eighteen to Earl Granville; and twenty-one to other persons; mainly relating to the restraint of American citizens in Ireland.

1884

Address | Delivered before the Birmingham and Midland Institute, | at Birmingham, | On Monday, Oc-

[99]

ADDRESS

DELIVERED BEFORE THE BIRMINGHAM AND MIDLAND INSTITUTE
AT BIRMINGHAM,

On Monday, October 6th, 1884.

BY

JAMES RUSSELL LOWELL, D.C.L.. LL.D., &c., &c.

TITLE-PAGE OF THE PRIVATE EDITION OF "ON DEMOCRACY"

[SIZE OF ORIGINAL]

tober 6th, 1884, | By | James Russell Lowell, D.C.L., LL.D., &c., &c.

Small 4to. Collation: Title, p. [1]; blank, p. [2]; text, pp. [2]–24, printed on recto only, verso of each leaf blank. Size of leaf, trimmed, 9¾6 by 7⅟₁₆ inches.

Issued stitched, without cover.

Consists of twenty-four leaves, signatures A, B, C, D, E, and F, each four leaves. There are no head-lines, the page-numbers being at the top in the center. At the bottom of p. 24 is the imprint "Harrison and Sons, Printers, St. Martin's Lane, London."

This first issue was printed off in London before Lowell left for Birmingham to deliver the address. Four copies are now traceable, two of which have corrections in Lowell's own autograph, and a third has similar corrections in another hand. Of the copies with autographic corrections, one, formerly in the possession of Mr. Hodgson, who was connected at the time with the American Embassy in London, was acquired by Mr. Chamberlain. A second, the one from which Mr. Lowell read the address, is owned by Wilson King of Birmingham, to whom it was presented by Lowell. A third, the William Harris Arnold copy, belongs to Dr. James B. Clemens; and the fourth, given by Lowell to Mr. Bowditch, belongs to Mr. Stephen H. Wakeman. In a letter to Mr. Chamberlain, dated April 27, 1902, Mr. King wrote:

"He made the marginal notes when sitting with Professor Mahaffy and me reading over his essay but at the same time joining in our conversation. He was in great spirits during the whole visit of five days and he and Dr. Mahaffy both sparkled and scintillated with fun all day. In the evenings we had dinner parties with the leading people of the neighborhood as guests when they had to be on their good behavior but the rest of the time they were like two jolly school boys out for a holiday." The corrections in the third copy, now in Dr. Clemens's collection, are in the autograph of Mr. Hodgson. The corrections in the King copy differ from the other two, which are practically identical.

At Mr. Chamberlain's request, a friend of his made an effort to secure the manuscript of the address from the printers, Harrison and Sons, and also to ascertain the exact number printed. In a letter dated June 6, 1902, he wrote:

"I next went to see Harrison. He said after the lapse of so many years he could not say anything about the matter, but it was their invariable custom to destroy all mss. not returned to the author, and as the order to print came from the U. S. embassy, it is quite likely the manuscript was returned to the embassy; That even though Mr. Lowell was long since dead, they would give no information concerning the number of copies printed (that is no certificate) as it would be a violation of a fixed principle, but after referring to his books, he told me that 500 copies were printed, and this, in *great primer,* and he assumed that they were not intended for circulation."

It is impossible, however, that so large a number was actually printed. Mr. King was under the impression that this earliest form was a "proof prepared for the London Times," and writes further, under date of July 7, 1902:

"As to the printing of the *first* edition, I feel pretty sure Mr. Lowell told me he had sent the ms. to the Times from which journal he had received the proof from which he read the address which I now have. Of course in that case any number of proofs may have been made, and Mr. Lowell may even have written on the margins of some copies (for friends) such small changes as he might recall having made."

The address appeared in the London *Times* probably the morning after its delivery. It also appeared in the *Pall Mall Budget* (a weekly) in the issue of October 10, 1884, with the following prefatory note: "In view, of the exceptional interest attaching to Mr. Lowell's inaugural address on Monday last as President of the Midland Institute we reproduce the American Minister's speech *in extenso.* Mr. Lowell's address, which has been specially revised by himself for these columns, was as follows:".

The text of the address as printed in these two periodicals has not been compared with this text or with that of the essay as published.

1884

Birmingham and Midland Institute. | [ornament] | On Democracy: | An Address | Delivered in the Town Hall, Birmingham, | On the 6th of October, 1884, | By | His Excellency, | The Hon. James Russell Lowell, | D.C.L., LL.D., | American Minister in London, | President. | [ornament] | Birmingham: | Printed by Cond Bros., Paternoster Row, | Moor Street.

8vo. Collation: Title and text, pp. [1]–15. Size of leaf, trimmed, 8½ by 5½ inches.

Issued stitched, without cover. There is another variety with "Price Sixpence." printed in the upper left-hand corner of the title-page.

Mr. Wilson King of Birmingham, who had been asked by Mr. Chamberlain as to the significance of the two editions, replied (in a letter dated July 7, 1902):

"I will enquire about the 'six pence' edition but I feel sure that that was the same as the Institute edition, a part of which was distributed gratuitously to members or subscribers whilst another part was sold to the general public at 6d per copy."

When originally sent out, a two-page circular of the Birmingham and Midland Institute, soliciting memberships, accompanied the pamphlet.

Since $110 was paid for a copy of this pamphlet at the William Harris Arnold sale in January, 1901, a considerable number of copies have come upon the market, secured partly from Cond Brothers, the printers, and partly from officials of the Birmingham and Midland Institute. When sending Mr. Chamberlain two copies, Mr. King wrote that the Institute still possessed ten copies, but that no more could be had from that source, as they usually made a point of keeping twelve copies of each presidential address.

"On Democracy" was collected with other addresses in the volume "Democracy and Other Addresses," published in the fall of 1886.

1884

Birmingham | Health Lectures, | with | Preface | by | His Excellency the Hon. James Russell Lowell | D.C.L., LL.D., | United States Minister in London; | President of the Birmingham and Midland Institute. | [rule] | Second Series. | [rule] | Birmingham: | Hudson and Son, Edmund Street. | London: | Hamilton, Adams, and Co., Paternoster Row. | [rule] | 1884.

12mo. Collation: Title, Contents, and Preface, pp. [i]–vii; text, pp. [1]–112. Imprint at bottom of p. 112, "Hudson and Son, Printers, Edmund Street, Birmingham."

Issued in gray paper cover, p. [1] reading: "Birmingham | Health Lectures | 1884: | With Preface by his Excellency | The Honourable James Russell Lowell, | [etc.] Price Ninepence." There are advertisements on pp. [2, 3, and 4] of cover, and ten pages of advertisements at back and front.

On pp. [v]–vii will be found the "Preface," signed "J. R. Lowell." and dated "January 5th, 1885."

1884

Browning Society. | [rule] | Monthly Abstract of Proceedings. | [rule] | Twenty-fourth Meeting, Friday, April 24, 1884.

8vo. Collation: 12 pp., numbered 113*–124*. Size of leaf, trimmed, 8%₁₆ by 5½ inches.
Issued stitched, without cover.

At this meeting Mr. Lowell occupied the chair and delivered an address on Browning, which fills line 5, p. 113* to line 9, p. 116*. There is a head-line on pp. 114* and 115*, "Mr. J. Russell Lowell on Browning's Works." A comment by Lowell on a paper by Mr. Morrison fills the lower two thirds of p. 124*.

The head-line of each page except the first is dated "April 4, 1884." while the date at the top of the first page is "April 24, 1884." Both dates are apparently incorrect, as in the collected form, where these Proceedings are reprinted, it is called the "Twenty-fourth Meeting Friday, April 25, 1884."

This "Monthly Abstract" is the earliest printed form. Later in the year it was reprinted in "The Browning Society's Papers 1881–4. Part V." Lowell's address is found on pp. 112*–115* of that part.

1884

[Double rule] | Transactions | of | The Wordsworth Society. | Edited by | The Hon. Secretary. | No. 6. | [double rule] | [Edinburgh, 1884.]

8vo. Collation: Title, Preface, and Contents, pp. [i–v]; half-title, text, half-title, and catalogue of Wordsworth's library, pp. [7]–257; photograph facing title. Size of leaf, trimmed, 8¾ by 5%₁₆ inches.

Issued in limp boards, cloth back, front cover lettered "Transactions | of the | Wordsworth | Society | No. VI. | Edinburgh: T. & A. Constable, Printers to her Majesty." Back cover lettered "It is requested that Members changing | their address will mention the fact to the | Secretary."

James Russell Lowell's address, as President of the Society, delivered May 10, 1884, is found on pp. 12–24. It was collected in the volume "Democracy and other Addresses," published late in 1886. In 1889 it was reprinted in the volume "Wordsworthiana, A Selection from Papers read to the Wordsworth Society," edited by William Knight.

1884

Emmanuel College | Cambridge | Commemoration | of the Three hundredth Anniversary | of | The Foundation | MDCCCLXXXIV

8vo. Collation: Half-title, imprint, and title, pp. [i–iii]; text, pp. [1]–99; imprint, p. [100]. Frontispiece portrait, separately printed. Size of leaf, untrimmed, 8¾ by 5¾ inches.

Issued in cloth, front cover lettered "Tercentenary Festival | of | Emmanuel College | Cambridge".

On pp. 9, 10 is a toast by Lowell: "Mr. Russell Lowell, who was received with | cheers, said: | 'It has been my good fortune to address many English | audiences. [etc.]' "

1884

Papers | Relating to the | Foreign Relations | of | The United States, | Transmitted to Congress, | With the Annual Message of the President, | December 4, 1883. | Prefaced by a | List of Papers and followed by an Index of | Persons and Subjects. | [rule] | Washington: | Government Printing Office. | 1884.

8vo. Collation: Title, Message, and List, pp. [i]–lxx; text and Index, pp. [1]–948. Size of leaf, trimmed, 9 by 5¾ inches.

Issued in cloth, back lettered "Foreign | Relations | of the | United | States | 1883".

This volume contains, on pp. 408–479, twenty-eight letters by Lowell, eighteen having been addressed to Mr. Frelinghuysen and eight to Earl Granville.

One of Lowell's communications to the Department of State was issued separately as a stitched pamphlet of 16 pp., with heading at top of p. 1, "Unclaimed Estates in England. | Mr. Lowell to the Secretary of State. | (No. 895) Legation of the United States, | London, November 15, 1884." It consists of a series of letters relative to claims for estates in England. Lowell's letter transmitting the others to the Secretary of State occupies p. [1].

In "Nathaniel Hawthorne and his Wife", Boston, 1884, there is printed (Vol. I, pp. 390–392) an interesting letter of Lowell's referring to Hawthorne's literary work.

1885

Celebration | of the | Two Hundred and Fiftieth Anniversary | of | The Incorporation | of | Concord, | September 12, 1885. | 1635–1885 | [ornament] | Concord, Mass.: | Published by the Town |

8vo. Collation: Title, imprint, Preface, and "At the General Court," etc., text, and Appendix, pp. [1–96]. Size of leaf, untrimmed, 9⅛ by 5⅞ inches.

Issued in blue paper covers, p. 1 printed from the types of the title-page. Also issued in cloth, back lettered "Celebration | at | Concord | Sept. 12, 1885. | 1635–1885"

This volume contains an address by Lowell on Concord in Literature, headed, "Mr. Lowell's Speech." Pp. 65–69. It has apparently never been collected.

1885

Wensley | And other Stories | By Edmund Quincy | Edited by his son, Edmund Quincy | [device] | Boston | James R. Osgood and Company | 1885

12mo. Collation: Title, copyright (dated 1885) and imprint, and Editor's Preface, pp. [i]–iv; "Bankside," pp. [v]–vii; Author's Preface, Contents, pp. [ix–xv]; half-title and text, pp. 1–349. Size of leaf, trimmed, 7⁹⁄₁₆ by 4⅞ inches.

Issued in red cloth, back lettered "Edmund | Quincy | Wensley | and | Other Stories | James R. Osgood & Co."

Edmund Quincy and James Russell Lowell were long intimate friends. In 1877 Lowell had written a poem, "Bankside," on the home of Quincy at Dedham. This was published in the *Nation* for May 31 of that year. It is prefixed to this volume of stories: "Bankside. | By James Russell Lowell. | May 21, 1877." Pp. [v]–vii. It was collected in the "Heartsease and Rue" volume in 1888.

1885

Proceedings | at | the presentation of a portrait | of | John Greenleaf Whittier | To Friends' School, Providence, R. I. | Tenth Month, 24th, 1884 | Cambridge | Printed at the Riverside Press | 1885

8vo. Collation: Title, Contents, pp. [i]–iv; text, pp. [1]–92. Portrait facing title, and plates facing pp. 1 and 92. Size of leaf, trimmed, 8½ by 5¾ inches.

Issued in paper covers, p. [1] reading: "Proceedings | at the presentation of a portrait of | John Greenleaf Whittier, to Friends' | School, Providence, R. I., Tenth Month, 24th, 1884".

Lowell's sonnet "To J. G. Whittier" is on p. 82. It was collected, with the title "To Whittier on his seventy-fifth Birthday," in "Heartsease and Rue," 1888. The sonnet is preceded by a letter addressed to Augustine Jones, Esq., signed "J. R. Lowell," dated "Legation of the United States | London, September 11, 1884."

1885

Papers | Relating to the | Foreign Relations | of | The United States. | Transmitted to Congress, | With the Annual Message of the President, | December 1, 1884, | Preceded by a | List of Papers and followed by an Index | of Persons and Subjects. | [device] | Washington: | Government Printing Office. | 1885.

8vo. Collation: Title, Message, and List, pp. [i]–lxx; text and Index, pp. [1]–619. Size of leaf, trimmed, 9 by 5¾ inches.

Issued in cloth, back lettered "Foreign | Relations | of the | United | States | 1884".

This volume contains ten letters by Lowell, occupying, with other correspondence, pp. 214–225. Seven were addressed to Mr. Frelinghuysen, the last, dated November 15, 1884, being his letter, with enclosure, relating to unclaimed estates in England, which was separately printed as described above (p. 106). Of the three other letters, two were addressed to Earl Granville, and one to Lord Northbrooke.

Three letters by Lowell were printed in "John Howard Payne, Dramatist, Poet, Actor, and Author of Home Sweet Home!" by Gabriel Harrison, Philadelphia, 1885. They refer to the removal of the remains of John Howard Payne to the United States, and had already been printed in "Foreign Relations of the United States," 1883.

Lowell was invited to deliver an address at the celebration of the two hundred and fiftieth anniversary of the settlement of Newbury, Mass., held on June 10, 1885. His letter declining the honor is printed on pp. 17 and 18 of the pamphlet published by the Historical Society, having the title: "Celebration of the Two Hundred and Fiftieth Anniversary of the Settlement of Newbury, June 10, 1885. Newburyport: Printed by order of the Historical Society of Old Newbury. MDCCCLXXXV."

In the "Proceedings of the Massachusetts Historical Society," Vol. I, Second Series, Boston, 1885, there is, on p. 229, a short letter from Lowell, dated "June 20, 1884."

1886

Proceedings | at the | Dedication | of the | New Library Building | Chelsea, Mass. | December 22, 1885 | With the | Address by James Russell Lowell | [device] | Cambridge | John Wilson and Son | University Press | 1886

8vo. Collation: Half-title, p. [i]; title and text, pp. [1–33]. Frontispiece. Size of leaf, trimmed, 9⅗ by 5⅞ inches.

Issued in boards, p. [1] printed from the types of the title-page.

This volume contains Lowell's Address on Books and Libraries: "Address. | By James Russell Lowell." Pp. 16–30. It was collected in "Democracy and Other Addresses," published late in 1886.

1886

Papers | Relating to the | Foreign Relations | of | The United States, | Transmitted to Congress, | With the Annual Message of the President, | December 8, 1885, | Preceded by a | List of Papers, with an Analysis of their Contents, and | followed by an Alphabetical Index of Subjects. | [device] | Washington: | Government Printing Office. | 1886.

8vo. Collation: Title, Message, and List, pp. [i]–c; text and Index, pp. [1]–950. Size of leaf, trimmed, 9 by 5¾ inches.

Issued in cloth, back lettered "Foreign | Relations | of the | United | States | 1885".

This volume contains, pp. 444–449, six letters from Lowell, two being to Mr. Frelinghuysen, one to his successor, Mr. Bayard, and three to Earl Granville. In June, 1885, Lowell returned to America.

1886

Fifth | Annual Report | of the | Dante Society. | May 18, 1886. | Appendix I. | Dante: James Russell Lowell. | Appendix II. | Dante, and the Lancelot Romance: | Paget Toynbee. | Cambridge: | John Wilson and Son. | University Press. | 1886.

8vo. Collation: Title, List of Officers, and text, pp. [1]–74. Size of leaf, trimmed, 9 by 6 inches.

Issued in paper cover, p. [1] printed from the types of the title-page. Other cover-pages blank.

This pamphlet contains: "Dante. | By James Russell Lowell. | Reprinted by consent of the Publishers from Appleton's | Cyclopaedia, 1859." Pp. 15–38.

This is an entirely different article from the essay "Dante" in the Second Series of "Among my Books."

1886

Democracy | and other Addresses | By | James Russell Lowell | [device] | Boston and New York | Houghton, Mifflin and Company | The Riverside Press, Cambridge | 1887

12mo. Collation: Blank, p. [1]; list of Lowell's writings, p. [2]; title, copyright (dated 1886) and imprint, Dedication, and Contents, pp. [i]–vi; half-title and text, pp. [1]–245. Size of leaf, untrimmed, 7¼ by 4¾ inches. Publishers' list bound in at end, pp. 1–14.

Issued in blue cloth, with paper label, "Democracy | and | Other Addresses | Lowell". Untrimmed copies in this form were issued as the first edition. Later bindings are different.

This volume contains nine addresses, of which five had already appeared in print elsewhere, as indicated:

"Democracy." Delivered in Birmingham, October 6, 1884. First printed as "On Democracy," London, 1884.

"Garfield." Delivered in London, September 24, 1881. First printed in the "Death of President Garfield," London, 1881.

"Stanley." Delivered in the Chapter House of Westminster Abbey, December 13, 1881.

"Fielding." Delivered at Taunton, England, September 4, 1883.

"Coleridge." Delivered in Westminster Abbey, May 7, 1885.

"Books and Libraries." Delivered at Chelsea, Mass., December 22, 1885. Printed in the "Proceedings at the Dedication of the New Library Building," 1886.

"Wordsworth." Delivered before the Wordsworth Society, Edinburgh, May 10, 1884. Printed in the "Transactions," No. VI, of the Society.

"Don Quixote." Read at the Workingmen's College in London, probably in 1885.

"Harvard University." Delivered at Cambridge, November 8, 1886. First printed in the *Atlantic Monthly* for December, 1886, and the next year in the Harvard Commemoration volumes.

Lowell was asked to assist in procuring a copy of a painting of Bishop Butler for presentation to Trinity College, Hartford; and a letter from him, dated "Legation of the United States, London, May 6, 1885," in reference to the matter, is printed on p. 6 of the pamphlet, "Speeches at the Presentation of the Portrait of Bishop Butler to Trinity College, on

Wednesday, June 23d, being the day before Commencement, 1886," Hartford, Conn., 1886.

The "Exercises of the Fiftieth Anniversary Commemorative of the Incorporation of the City of Lowell," Lowell, 1886, contains, on p. 83, a letter from J. R. Lowell, dated January 25, 1886, in which he expresses his regret at his inability to attend the celebration.

The "Proceedings of the Dedication of the Fountain on Eaton Square, in Memory of Theodore Lyman, Jr.," Boston, 1886, contains Lowell's poem "The Fountain," set to music. The poem itself was first published in "Poems," 1844. The same volume contains, on p. 54, a three-line letter from Lowell, dated "Southborough, Mass., Oct. 23, 1885."

1887

1636. Harvard University. 1886. | [rule] | A Record of the Commemoration, | November Fifth to Eighth, 1886, | on the | Two Hundred and Fiftieth Anniversary | of the | Founding of Harvard College. | [device] | Cambridge, N. E.: | John Wilson and Son. | University Press. | 1887.

Large 8vo. Collation: Half-title, title, Records, text, half-title, and Registration, pp. [1]–379. Facsimiles facing title and p. 11. Size of leaf, untrimmed, 10 by 6½ inches.

Issued in cloth, back lettered "Harvard College | 250th Anniversary | 1886".

This volume contains two pieces by Lowell:
(1) "Oration. | By James Russell Lowell." Pp. 194–236.
(2) "Speech of James Russell Lowell." Pp. 300–302.
The first of these was included in the volume "Democracy and other Addresses," published late in 1886. The second, shorter speech apparently has not been reprinted.

1887

Richard The Third | and | The Primrose Criticism | [quotation, 3 lines]. | Chicago | A. C. McClurg and Company | 1887

16mo. Collation: half-title, title, copyright (dated 1887), quotation from Lowell's address, and Contents, pp. [1–7]; half-title and text, pp. [9]–164. Size of leaf, untrimmed, 7⅛ by 4¾ inches.

Issued in cloth, back lettered "Richard | The | Third. | A. C. McClurg | & Co."

On p. [5] is an extract, fourteen lines, from Lowell's address on Shakespeare's "Richard III" before the Union League Club in Chicago, signed "James Russell Lowell, | Chicago, Feb. *22*, 1887." This address had been delivered before the Edinburgh Philosophical Institution in 1883, but was not collected until 1891, when it was included in the volume "Latest Literary Essays and Addresses." The extract from the Chicago address differs slightly from the corresponding passage in the lecture as collected. The book itself was written by the Rev. Frank M. Bristol.

1887

The West Church, Boston | [rule] | Commemorative Services | on the | fiftieth Anniversary of its present | Ministry | and the | One hundred and fiftieth of its | foundation | On Tuesday, March 1, 1887 | With three sermons by its Pastor | With Illustrations | Boston | Damrell and Upham | 1887

8vo. Collation: Half-title, title, imprint, Contents, Illustrations, Prefatory Note, half-title, pp. [1–11]; text, pp. [13]–124. Plates, separately printed, facing title and pp. 16, 18, 20, 56, 84. Size of leaf, untrimmed, 9¼ by 6⅛ inches.

Issued in cloth, lettered "Commemorative | Services | at | West Church | Boston | 1737–1887 |."

This volume contains: "Address of James Russell Lowell, | D.C.L., LL.D." Pp. 58–64. This seems never to have been collected.

1887

Proceedings | of the | Massachusetts Historical Society, | from | October, 1886, to January, 1887 | (Inclusive).

8vo. Collation: No title-page, above being p. [1] of cover; text, pp. 55–205. Size of leaf, untrimmed, 9⅝ by 6¾₁₆ inches.

Issued in gray paper cover. P. [1] as above; pp. [2–4] blank.

On pp. 149–152 is Mr. Lowell's tribute to Charles Francis Adams, beginning with: "The Hon. James Russell Lowell followed with these | words:— | 'The leading traits of our late associate's character were so emphatic,'" etc.

1888

Reform Club Series.—I | [rule] | The Independent in Politics | An Address delivered before the Reform Club | of New York, April 13, 1888 | By | James Russell Lowell | [rule] | New York | The Reform Club | 12 East 33d Street | 1888

8vo. Collation: Title, copyright (dated 1888) and imprint, and text, pp. [i]–27. Size of leaf, small paper, trimmed, 8 by 5¼ inches; large paper, untrimmed, 9¾ by 7¼ inches.

Issued in blue paper cover, p. [1] reading "Reform Club Series.—I | [rule] | The Independent in Politics | James Russell Lowell | [rule] | The Reform Club, New York".

The large-paper issue, 300 copies, has a notice on p. 2: "Large Paper Edition | 300 Copies. No. ....".

This address was delivered April 13, 1888, and was printed in the New York *Evening Post* for April 17, 1888; also in the *Civil Service Reformer*, published in Baltimore, in the number for May, 1888. It was printed the same year by G. P. Putnam's Sons, as No. XLVIII of their "Questions of the Day" series; and was collected in the volume "Political Essays," published in July, 1888.

1888

Political Essays | By | James Russell Lowell | [device] | Boston and New York | Houghton, Mifflin and Company | The Riverside Press, Cambridge | 1888

12mo. Collation: Title, copyright (dated 1888) and imprint, Prefatory Note, and Contents, pp. [i–v]; text, pp. [1]–326. Size of leaf, untrimmed, 7⅞ by 5 inches.

Issued in blue cloth with paper label, "Political Essays | Lowell | First Edition".

Only seventy-five copies were bound up, entirely untrimmed, and with label reading, "First Edition," as described above.

This volume contains thirteen pieces, all but one of which had previously appeared in either the *Atlantic Monthly* or the *North American Review*, and which had not before been collected. The contents of the volume, and the first appearance of the several essays, are as follows:

"The American Tract Society." *Atlantic Monthly*, July, 1858.

"The Election in November." *Atlantic Monthly*, October, 1860.

"E Pluribus Unum." *Atlantic Monthly*, February, 1861.

"The Pickens and Stealin's Rebellion." *Atlantic Monthly*, June, 1861.

"General McClellan's Report." *North American Review*, April, 1864.

"The Rebellion, its Causes and Consequences." *North American Review*, July, 1864.

"McClellan or Lincoln?" *North American Review*, October, 1864.

"Abraham Lincoln." As "The President's Policy." *North American Review*, January, 1864. Also printed as a pamphlet, 1864.

"Reconstruction." *North American Review*, April, 1865.

"Scotch the Snake, or Kill it?" *North American Review*, July, 1865.

"The President on the Stump." *North American Review*, April, 1866.

"The Seward-Johnson Reaction." *North American Review*, October, 1866.

"The Place of the Independent in Politics." *New York Evening Post*, April 17, 1888. Also separately as a pamphlet.

1888

Heartsease and Rue | By | James Russell Lowell | [publishers' device] | Boston and New York | Houghton, Mifflin and Company | The Riverside Press, Cambridge | 1888

12mo. Collation: Blank, p. [1]; list of Lowell's writings, p. [2]; title, copyright (dated 1888) and imprint, quotation (4 lines), Contents, and half-title, pp. [i–ix]; text, pp. [i]–218; engraved portrait facing title. Size of leaf, untrimmed, 7³⁄₁₆ by 4⁷⁄₈ inches.

Issued in blue cloth, with paper label, "Heartsease | and | Rue | Lowell". Also in gray boards, white cloth back, lettered in gilt "Heartsease | and Rue | J. R. Lowell | Houghton | Mifflin & Co."

The concluding line on p. 63, "That women in their self-surrender know?" was omitted in a few copies. A copy exists with this line in Lowell's autograph.

This was the last collection of verse published during the author's life. Some of the poems included had been printed in the *Atlantic Monthly, Harper's Magazine,* and the *Nation,* but a number of pieces are here printed for the first time. Two hundred and fifty copies were issued in blue cloth with paper label.

1888

The English Poets: | Lessing, Rousseau: | Essays by James Russell | Lowell, with "An Apology | For a Preface." | London | Walter Scott, 24 Warwick Lane | Toronto: W. J. Gage and Co. | 1888

16mo. Collation: Half-title, title, Contents, Apology, pp. [i]–x; text, pp. [11]–337. Publishers' list bound in at end, pp. [1–6]. Size of leaf, trimmed, 6⅝ by 4⅝ inches.

Issued in red cloth, back lettered in gilt "Essays on the | English Poets | J. R. Lowell | [in black] Camelot | Series | Walter Scott".

The essays had been printed long before, but the "Apology for a Preface," pp. vii–x, was written especially for this edition. It is dated at end, "October 13th, 1888."

1888

The History | of the | World's Progress. | A General History of the Earth's Construction, and | of the Advancement of Mankind. | With an Introduction by Hon. James Russell Lowell. | Edited by | Charles E. Beale, A.M., LL.B. | Vol. I [II] | World's Library Association: | 592 Washington St., Boston, Mass. | [1888]

2 vols., large 8vo. Collation, Vol. I: Title, p. [i]; copyright (dated 1886), p. [ii]; Introduction by Lowell, pp. [i]–x; List of

Illustrations, pp. [iii]–vii; text, pp. [1]–600. Vol. II: Title, p. [i]; text, pp. 601–1088; Contents, pp. 1089–1108. Size of leaf, trimmed, 11½ by 8⅞ inches.

Issued in stamped cloth, marbled edges, back lettered "History | of the | World's | Progress. | Vol. I | Illustrated." Probably issued also in leather binding.

This is the second edition of the book, not published until 1888. The first edition of 1886 did not contain Lowell's Introduction, which was printed later and interpolated between pp. [ii] and [iii]. Lowell's Introduction was collected in "Latest Literary Essays," 1891.

1888

Proceedings | at the | Meeting for the Formation | of | The International Copyright | Association, | Parker House, December 27, 1887. | [ornament] | Boston: | Press of Rockwell and Churchill, 39 Arch Street. | 1888.

8vo. Collation: Title, Object of Corporation, and text, pp. [1]–23. Size of leaf, trimmed, 8½ by 6 inches.
Issued stitched, without cover.

Remarks by Lowell, prefaced by "Mr. Lowell took the chair and said:", occupy pp. 11, 12.

1888

What American Authors Think | About International Copyright. | [ornament] | New-York | American Copyright League | 1888.

8vo. Collation: Title, facsimile of a letter from Longfellow, and text, pp. [1–16]. Size of leaf, trimmed, 9⁹⁄₁₆ by 6¹¹⁄₁₆ inches.
Issued stitched, without cover.

On p. [3] is a facsimile of Lowell's verses on copyright (four lines), signed "J. R. Lowell" and dated "20th Nov: 1885." This same facsimile appears in several later publications of the American Copyright League.

On pp. 10 and 11 is an extract from a "Statement before the Senate Committee on Patents, Friday, January 29, 1886," thirty-seven lines, signed "James Russell Lowell"; and filling pp. 14 and 15 is "An Open Letter to Readers of Books. | Address of the American Copyright League, January, 1888.", signed "James Russell Lowell, President. | E. C. Stedman, Vice President," and five other names, members of the Executive Committee.

1888

Report of the Proceedings | at the dinner | given by | the Society of Authors | To | American Men and Women of Letters | at the Criterion Restaurant, | on Wednesday, July 25, 1888. | [double rule] | London: | Society of Authors, | 4, Portugal Street, Lincoln's Inn Fields, W. C. | 1888.

8vo. Collation: No title-page, above being on p. [1] of cover. Pp. [1–2] blank; text, pp. 3–47; imprint, "Billing and Sons, Printers, Guildford.", at bottom of p. 47. Size of leaf, trimmed, 9⅝ by 6⅛ inches.

Issued in gray paper cover, p. [1] as above; p. [2] blank; p. [3] List of Officers; p. 4 blank.

Lowell's address, on pp. 18–25, is headed: "Mr. J. Russell Lowell, who was received with loud applause, said:" etc.

"Arbor Day, Edited and Compiled by Robert W. Furnas," published in Lincoln, Nebraska, in 1888, contains, on pp. 102–104, a letter from Lowell, dated "Deerfoot Farm, Southborough, Mass., March 25, 1888."

1889

Address | By | James Russell Lowell, D.C.L., LL.D. | Before the | Modern Language Association of America | 1889 | [rule] | Extracted from the | Publications of the Modern Language Association, | Vol. V, No. 1.

8vo. Collation: No title-page, above being on p. 1 of cover; text, pp. [5]–22, with heading on p. [5]: "Address.* | By James Russell Lowell, D.C.L., LL.D., | Cambridge, Mass." At the bottom of p. [5] is: "*Copyright, 1890, by James Russell Lowell." Size of leaf, untrimmed, 9 by 6⅛ inches.

Issued in paper cover, p. [1] as above. Other cover-pages blank.

The cover-title, as above, says that the address was "Extracted from the Publications of the Modern Language Association, Vol. V, No. 1," and it is probable that that volume was first published, but this form is certainly the more desirable. The other pamphlet has the following title-page:

"Vol. V, No. 1. | Publications | of the | Modern Language Association | of America | January–March | [rule] | Baltimore: | 1890." It has thirty-two pages of text, Lowell's address occupying pp. 5–22.

1889

Library of Tribune Extras. | Vol. I. May, 1889. No. 5. | The Washington Centenary | Celebrated in New-York | April 29, 30–May 1, 1889. | [vignette] | President Harrison entering the City Hall—View from the Tribune Building. | [rule] | $2 a year. Single Copies, 25 cents. | [rule] | The Tribune Association, | New-York.

8vo. Collation: No title-page, above being p. [1] of cover; Illustrations, pp. [i–viii]; text, pp. [1]–120. Size of leaf, trimmed, 10 by 6¾ inches.

Issued in paper cover, p. [1] as above; pp. [2, 3] blank; p. [4] advertisements.

On pp. 71, 72, are some extracts from Lowell's address, beginning: "Remarks by Mr. Lowell. | Here are some of the points made by James | Russell Lowell in his address."

1889

The | Complete Angler, | or the | Contemplative Man's Recreation, | of | Izaak Walton and Charles Cotton. |

With an Introduction | By James Russell Lowell. | Vol. I. [Vol. II.] | [vignette] | Boston: | Little, Brown, and Company. | 1889.

2 vols., 8vo. Collation: Vol. I: Half-title, title, number of copies printed, copyright (dated 1889) and imprint, Contents, List of Embellishments, Introduction, half-title, Dedication, and To all Readers, pp. [i]–lxxvi; text, pp. 1–208. Plates, separately printed, facing title and pp. 1, 66, 149, 159, 176, 202, 206. Vol. II: Half-title, title, number of copies printed, copyright and imprint, and Contents, pp. [i]–vi; text, half-title, and Index, pp. 208–456. Plates, separately printed, facing title and pp. 263, 296, 305, 339, 350, and 394. Size of leaf, untrimmed, 8 by 5⅛ inches.

Issued in green cloth, gilt ornaments, back lettered "The | Complete | Angler | Walton & Cotton | Vol. I. [Vol. II.] | Little, Brown & Co." One hundred and fifty copies were printed on large paper. These were bound in boards.

Lowell's Introduction, written especially for this edition, fills pp. [xv]–lxv. It was reprinted in "Latest Literary Essays and Addresses," 1892.

1889

Life of | Harriet Beecher Stowe | Compiled from | Her Letters and Journals | By her Son | Charles Edward Stowe | [device] | Boston and New York | Houghton, Mifflin and Company | The Riverside Press, Cambridge | 1890

8vo. Collation: Title, copyright (dated 1889), Introductory Statement, Contents, and List of Illustrations, pp. [i]–xii; text and Index, pp. [1]–530; List of Works, pp. [531–536]. Facsimile manuscript preface, two leaves, following title; other illustrations as given in list on pp. [xi]–xii. Size of leaf, trimmed, 8⅝ by 5⅝ inches.

Issued in blue cloth, gilt top, back lettered "Life of | Harriet

Beecher | Stowe | Charles E. Stowe | Illustrated | Houghton | Mifflin and Co."

Lowell's appreciation of "The Minister's Wooing" is on pp. 327–332, and a long letter from him, dated "Cambridge, February 4, 1859," is on pp. 333–336.

1890

Areopagitica | A Speech of Mr. John Milton | for | The Liberty of Unlicensed Printing, | To the Parliament of England | With an Introduction by | James Russell Lowell | [Grolier Club device] | New-York | The Grolier Club | MDCCCXC

16mo. Collation: Number of copies printed, half-title, title, half-title, copyright (dated 1890), Introduction, and title of first edition, pp. [i]–lx; text, pp. [1]–189. Etched portrait, separately printed, facing title. Size of leaf, untrimmed, 6⁹⁄₁₆ by 4⁵⁄₁₆ inches.

Issued in blue boards, with paper label, "Areopagitica | John Milton".

The Introduction by Lowell fills pp. [xi]–lvii. It was reprinted in the volume "Latest Literary Essays and Addresses," 1892.

1890

The Soldier's Field | Henry Lee Higginson | Major, First Massachusetts Cavalry | Brevet Lieutenant Colonel, U. S. V. |

8vo. Collation: Title, p. [i]; Military Order of the Loyal Legion, etc., pp. [iii–vi]; half-title, p. 1; text, pp. [3]–12. Size of leaf, trimmed, 9¼ by 5¾ inches.

Issued in paper cover, p. [1] reading, "The Soldier's Field | Henry Lee Higginson".

Lowell's inscription for a stone for the field is on p. 9:
"To the | Happy Memory | of | James Savage, Jr., | Charles Russell

Lowell, | Edward Barry Dalton, | Stephen George Perkins, | James Jackson Lowell, | Robert Gould Shaw, | Friends, Comrades, Kinsmen, who died for their | Country, | This Field is Dedicated."

1890

My Brook. | Words | By | James Russell Lowell | Drawings | By | Wilson de Meza | Supplement to the New York Ledger | December 13th 1890

Folio. Collation: 2 leaves, the above title on p. [19]; the poem and illustrations on pp. 20 and 21; and on p. [22], within a scroll, "Souvenir | The | New York | Ledger | Supplement | Dec 13 1890."

This supplement, issued separately and not stitched in, is described, although it is paged continuously with the weekly paper which it accompanied. A poem by Whittier, "The Captain's Well," was issued as a similar supplement to the *Ledger* of an earlier date. Some copies of that supplement were bound in stamped paper boards, but this poem of Lowell's was apparently never issued in covers.

"My Brook" is not included in the collected editions of Lowell's poems, but it is reprinted in Edward Everett Hale's "James Russell Lowell and his Friends," 1899.

The Riverside Edition of "The Writings of James Russell Lowell in Prose and Poetry," published in 1890, contains some material collected for the first time. Though edited by Lowell himself, he made few if any revisions, and the text was mainly reprinted from earlier volumes. Vols. I to VI are Prose, and Vols. VII to X, Poetry.

Vol. I contains a "Prefatory Note to the Essays," dated at end "25th April, 1890."

Vol. VI, "Literary and Political Addresses," contains two essays here first collected:

"Tariff Reform. Address at a Meeting of the Tariff Reform League, Boston, December 29, 1887."

"'Our Literature.' Response to a Toast at the Banquet in New York, April 30, 1889." Selections from this appeared in the "Tribune Extra," 1889.

Vol. VII contains a "Prefatory Note to the Poems," dated "9th May, 1890," and a rhymed "Letter from Boston," dated December, 1846, filling pp. 305–312. This piece had been printed in the *Anti-Slavery Standard* in 1848 and again in the *Atlantic Monthly* in 1884, but is here first collected.

Vol. IX contains "Fragments of an Unfinished Poem," filling pp. 126–136. This was reprinted from *Putnam's Monthly* for April, 1853.

"The Story of The Memorial Fountain to Shakespeare at Stratford-upon-Avon", Cambridge, The Riverside Press, 1890, contains, on pp. 35–38, a letter from Lowell, beginning, "Dear Sir Arthur Hodgson", and signed "J. R. Lowell" but undated. The fountain was the gift of George W. Childs of Philadelphia.

In "The Art of Authorship, Literary Reminiscences, Methods of Work," etc., edited by George Bainton, is an extract from a letter by Lowell, but without date or signature. It is on pp. 29, 30.

An eight-page pamphlet, made up of testimonials and notices of Melville D. Landon's "Wise, Witty, Eloquent Kings of the Platform and Pulpit," published in Chicago in 1890, contains, on p. 4, a letter from Lowell, without date but with signature in facsimile.

1891

Latest Literary Essays | And Addresses | of | James Russell Lowell | [device] | Cambridge | Printed at the Riverside Press | 1891.

8vo. Collation: Half-title, title, copyright (dated 1891) and limit notice, Note, and Contents, pp. [i–vii]; text, pp. [1]–184. Portrait facing title. Size of leaf, untrimmed, 8⅞ by 5⅞ inches.

Issued in gray boards, white cloth back, with paper label, "Lowell's | Writings | Latest | Literary Essays | And Addresses | Large Paper".

The above is a description of the large-paper edition, dated 1891. The regular edition, dated 1892, has list of Lowell's works preceding title instead of half-title, and has imprint: "Boston and New York | Houghton, Mifflin and Company | The Riverside Press, Cambridge | 1892." It was issued in cloth, lettered "Lowell's | Prose | Works | Latest | Literary | Essays | Houghton | Mifflin & Co".

Lowell died on August 12, 1891. This volume was made up by his lifelong friend and literary executor, Charles Eliot Norton. There is an introductory Note by him dated "Cambridge, Massachusetts, 16 November, 1891." The seven essays in the volume had all appeared in print before; those on Walton, Milton's "Areopagitica," and "The Progress of the World," having first appeared as introductions to other volumes, as already described.

"Portraits and Autographs: An Album for the People," London, 1891, contains a facsimile of a letter by Lowell, dated "Elmwood, Cambridge, Mass. 28th Jan: 1890."

1892

The | Old English Dramatists | By | James Russell Lowell | [Publishers' device] | Cambridge Printed at the Riverside Press | 1892

8vo. Collation: Half-title, title, copyright (dated 1892), limit notice, Note, and Contents, pp. [i–vii]; text, pp. [1]–132. Portrait facing title. Size of leaf, untrimmed, 8⅞ by 6 inches.

Issued in gray boards, cloth back, with paper label, "Lowell's | Writings | Old English | Dramatists | Large Paper."

The regular issue has list of Lowell's works, verso of leaf preceding title, instead of half-title, and has imprint "Boston and New York | Houghton, Mifflin and Company | The Riverside Press, Cambridge | 1892." It was issued in cloth, some copies being lettered "Lowell's | Prose | Works | Old English | Dramatists | Houghton | Mifflin & Co."

The six lectures which make up this volume appeared in *Harper's Magazine*, June to November, 1892.

1892

American | Ideas | For | English Readers | By James Russell Lowell | With Introduction by | Henry Stone | Published by | J. G. Cupples Co, | 250 Boylston St. | Boston

12mo. Collation: Half-title, title, copyright (dated 1892), Contents, and Introduction, pp. [i–xv]; text, pp. [1]–94. Portrait facing title. Publishers' lists bound in at end, pp. [1–8]. Size of leaf, trimmed, 6¹⁵⁄₁₆ by 3¹³⁄₁₆ inches.

Issued in cloth, front cover lettered "American Ideas | For | English Readers | Lowell."

This volume contains eleven addresses delivered in England from November 6, 1880, to December 23, 1888. It was made up from newspaper reports and was unauthorized.

In "Abraham Coles: Biographical Sketch . . . Edited by his Son Jonathan Ackerman Coles," New York, 1892, there is, on p. [276], a short comment, nine lines, by Lowell.

1893

Conversations | On Some of | The Old Poets. | By | James Russell Lowell. | With an Introduction | By | Robert Ellis Thompson, S.T.D. | [rule] | [quotation, 4 lines] | [rule] | Third Edition Enlarged. | [rule] | Philadelphia: | David McKay, Publisher, | 23 South Ninth Street. | 1893.

12mo. Collation: Quotation, 8 lines, p. [2]; title, copyright (dated 1893), Dedication, quotation, 7 lines, Editor's Introduction, and To the Reader, pp. [i]–xiv; text, pp. 1–294. 1 leaf of publisher's advertisement at end. Size of leaf, trimmed, 7¼ by 5 inches.

Issued in cloth, gilt top, back lettered "The | Old Poets | Lowell | American Classic | Series".

This edition contains two essays: "The Plays of Thomas Middleton," pp. 243–270, and "Song-Writing," pp. 271–294, not in the Second Edition of 1846. These two articles had appeared in the *Pioneer* in 1843, the first in No. I, the second in No. II of that short-lived periodical.

1893

Letters of | James Russell Lowell | Edited by | Charles Eliot Norton | Volume I. [Volume II.] | [Publishers' device] | New York | Harper & Brothers Publishers | 1894

2 vols., 8vo. Collation: Vol. I: Title, copyright (dated 1893), Editorial Note, and Contents, pp. [i]–viii; text, pp. 1–418. Portrait facing title. Vol. II: Title, copyright, and Contents, pp. [i]–v; text and Index, pp. 1–464. Portrait facing title. Size of leaf, untrimmed, 8¾ by 5¾ inches.

Issued in blue buckram, back lettered "Letters of | James Russell | Lowell | Charles Eliot Norton | I. [II.] | Harper & Brothers".

An extract from a letter to Mrs. Francis G. Shaw, beginning "My dear Sarah:", printed on pp. 195, 196 of Vol. I, was reprinted privately as a remembrance card, probably late in 1893, after the publication of these volumes. This extract was printed in black-letter type, with the initial letter in red, upon heavy cardboard, with beveled edges. The card measures 9¾₁₆ by 7⅛ inches.

1894

The Harvard Crimson | Supplement, containing unpublished fragments, furnished by Charles Eliot | Norton, from the College Lectures of | James Russell Lowell. | Copyrighted by E. H. Warren | for the Harvard Crimson | Cambridge, Mass. Friday, March 23, 1894. | Price 5 Cents.

Large 8vo. Six supplements were issued. The above is the heading of p. [1] of the first. Others are dated March 30, April 13, 20, and 27, and May 4, 1894. Each consists of 4 pp. with text in three columns. Portions of pp. [3, 4] of each issue are occupied by publisher's lists.

The following articles by Lowell, mainly selections from his lectures, are included:

No. I.
"The Study of Literature."
"The Study of Modern Languages."
No. II.
"Translation."
"Originality and Tradition in Literature."
"Choice in Reading."
"Books and Libraries."
No. III.
"The Search for Truth."
Close of Lecture at Cornell University.
No. IV.
"Elements of the English Language."

No. V.
"The Poetic and the Actual."
"Poetry in Homely Lines."
"The Practical and the Ideal."
"Style."
"Piers Ploughman."
"Montaigne."
"A Criticism of Wordsworth."

No. VI.
"The Humorous and the Comic."
"First Need of American Culture."
Harvard Anniversary. This is a part of Lowell's address on the 250th anniversary of Harvard.

1895

Last Poems | of | James Russell Lowell | [Publishers'
device] | Boston and New York | Houghton, Mifflin
and Company | The Riverside Press, Cambridge |
M DCCC XCV

12mo. Collation: Title, copyright (dated 1895) and imprint,
Note, Contents, and text, pp. [1]–47, printed on recto only. Portrait facing title. Size of leaf, untrimmed, 7½ by 5 inches.

Issued in cloth, back lettered "Last | Poems | James | Russell |
Lowell | Houghton | Mifflin & Co".

The Explanatory Note, signed "C. E. N[orton]," is dated "September,
1895."

1895

The | Poems of John Donne | From the text of the edi-
tion of 1633 | Revised By | James Russell Lowell |
With the various readings | of the other editions of
the Seventeenth Century, and | With a Preface, an
Introduction, and Notes by | Charles Eliot Norton |
Volume I [Volume II] | [Grolier Club device] | New-
York | The Grolier Club | 1895

2 vols., 16mo. Collation: Vol. I: Number of copies printed,
half-title, title, copyright (dated 1895), Preface, Contents, Introduction, and Note, pp. [i–xxxix]; half-title, text, half-title, notes,
and Corrigenda, pp. 1–[255]; imprint, p. [256]. Portrait facing
title, separately printed. Vol. II: Half-title, title, copyright
(dated 1895), Contents, and note, pp. [iii]–xi; half-title, text,
half-title, notes, and Corrigenda, pp. 1–287; imprint, p. [288].
Portrait facing title. Size of leaf, untrimmed, 6⅞ by 4¾ inches.

Issued in gray cloth, back lettered "Poems | of | John |
Donne | [device] | Volume I."

1896

The Power of | Sound | A Rhymed | Lecture by | James Russell Lowell | Privately | Printed | New York | MDCCCXCVI

8vo. Collation: Blank, pp. [i–ii]; half-title, copyright (dated 1896), half-title, Introductory Note, and half-title, pp. [iii–xi]; text and notes, pp. 1–35; colophon, p. [36]. Size of leaf, untrimmed, 8 by 5⅝ inches.

Issued in boards, cloth back and corners, back lettered "The | Power | of | Sound | Lowell | New York | 1896".

This edition was printed from a unique copy preserved in the form of a galley-proof, printed probably in 1857 or shortly thereafter, and used by Lowell in the delivery of the lecture. Lowell introduced a few passages from it into "Mason and Slidell" in 1862; but though delivered several times as a lecture, the poem was never published by him. The Introductory Note is by Charles Eliot Norton. This edition consisted of twenty-five copies on Japan paper and fifty on hand-made paper, and was printed at the expense of the late Edwin B. Holden.

1897

Lectures | on | English Poets | By | James Russell Lowell | "—Call up him who left half-told | The story of Cambuscan Bold." | [ornament] | Cleveland | The Rowfant Club | M DCCC XCVII

8vo. Collation: Number of copies printed, title, copyright (dated 1897), Contents, and Introduction, pp. [i]–xvi; half-title and text, pp. [1]–210; imprint, p. 211. Size of leaf, untrimmed, 8⅞ by 5¹⁵⁄₁₆ inches.

Issued in half-binding, cloth sides, leather back, lettered "Lectures | on | English | Poets | Lowell | The | Rowfant | Club".

These lectures were delivered in Boston before the Lowell Institute in January and February, 1855. They are here reprinted from reports printed at the time in the *Boston Daily Advertiser*. The Introduction by

S. A. J[ones] is dated "Ann Arbor, November 10th, 1896." 224 copies were printed.

W. J. Stillman was a friend of Lowell, and in his "The Old Rome and the New," London, 1897, there is a chapter, "A Few of Lowell's Letters." Eleven letters are printed but they had been for the most part included in "Letters," 1894. An extract from a letter of May 14, 1857, printed on pp. 155–156, and a portion of a letter of March 7, 1882, on p. 161, only, seem to be here first printed.

Lowell's poem "The Singing Leaves," which had been printed in "Under the Willows" in 1868, was set to music by Grace Mayhew and published in Boston by the H. B. Stevens Company in 1897. The composer took some slight liberties with Lowell's text.

In the "Proceedings of the Massachusetts Historical Society, Second Series, Vol. XI, 1897," Boston, 1897, there is printed on pp. 208, 209, "An extract from a despatch dated at Madrid, February 6, 1878, and sent to the State Department in Washington by the Honorable James Russell Lowell," twenty-five lines.

In "John Sullivan Dwight, Brook-Farmer, Editor, and Critic of Music," by George Willis Cooke, Boston, 1898, are printed two letters from Lowell. One of these, relating to contributions to the *Pioneer,* is on p. 70; the other, telling of an interview with Asa Gray, on pp. 105–107.

In the "Sources of the History of Oregon," edited by F. G. Young, Secretary of the Oregon Historical Society, issued in parts beginning in 1897, Part 3 of Vol. I, printed at Eugene, Oregon, in 1899, contains on p. [iii] an extract from a letter written by Lowell, addressed "Dear Miss H. . . ." and dated "Elmwood, Cambridge, Mass., 24th April, 1890.", sixteen lines, referring to Lowell's recollections of Captain Wyeth.

1899

James Russell Lowell | and His Friends | By | Edward Everett Hale | With Portraits, Facsimiles, and other | Illustrations | [Publishers' device] | Boston and New York | Houghton, Mifflin and Company | The Riverside Press, Cambridge | 1899

8vo. Collation: Title, copyright (dated 1898 and 1899), Contents, and Illustrations, pp. [i]–viii; text and Index, pp. [1]–303; imprint, p. 304. Illustrations, separately printed, facing title and pp. 4, 8, 12, 18, 36, 50, 52, 74, 78, 84, 86, 92, 96, 112, 114, 134, 138, 150, 154, 158, 162, 164, 168, 178, 182, 184, 186, 188, 196, 198, 202, 210, 240, 258, 266, 268, 270, 274, 284. Size of leaf, untrimmed, 8$\frac{11}{16}$ by 5$\frac{15}{16}$ inches.

Issued in cloth, back lettered "James | Russell | Lowell | and | His Friends | Edward | Everett | Hale | Houghton | Mifflin & Co."

Facing p. 50 is a reproduction of the broadside, "To the Class of '38," and between pp. 284 and 285 is a reproduction of the first two stanzas and the last stanza of "My Brook." The latter poem is printed entire on pp. 285, 286. Other uncollected verses first printed here are found on pp. 34, 38, and 39.

1899

Specimens | of | Printing | Types | in use at the | Marion Press | Jamaica, Queensborough | New-York | [rule] | Together with a List of | the Publications of | the Marion Press | [device] | September | 1899

8vo. Collation: Title, woodcut, Prefatory Note, quotation, and specimens, pp. [1–18]; Publications of the Marion Press, p. [19]; blank, p. [20].

Issued stitched, without cover. The title is within an ornamental frame, which is printed in blue ink. Size of leaf, untrimmed, 9$\frac{1}{8}$ by 6$\frac{1}{8}$ inches.

On p. [9] there are printed a letter from J. R. Lowell, dated "10, Lowndes Square, S.W., March 18, 1881," and a little poem, three stanzas of five lines each, with title "Cuiviscunque." and signed "Quivis," which had been sent with the letter.

Three hundred copies of these "Specimens" were printed.

"Impressions of Spain James Russell Lowell Compiled by Joseph B. Gilder," Boston, 1899, is made up of selections from Lowell's letters to the Department of State, printed in "Papers Relating to the Foreign Relations of the United States," 1878–79.

1901

James Russell Lowell | A Biography | By | Horace Elisha Scudder | In Two Volumes | Volume I [Volume II] | [Publishers' device] | Cambridge | Printed at the Riverside Press | MCMI

2 vols., 8vo. Collation: Vol. I: Half-title, title, copyright (dated 1901), limit notice, Dedication, Preface, and List of Illustrations, pp. [i–xiii]; text, pp. [1]–455; imprint on p. 456. Portraits and plates facing title and pp. 10, 116, 306, 360, and 384. Vol. II: Half-title, title, copyright and limit notice, Contents, and List of Illustrations, pp. [i–vii]; text, Appendix, and Index, pp. 1–482; imprint on p. 483. Portrait facing title; plates facing pp. 64, 120, 186, 318, 394. Size of leaf, untrimmed, 8$\frac{13}{16}$ by 5$\frac{15}{16}$ inches.

Issued in gray boards, cloth back, with paper label, "James | Russell | Lowell | A Biography | I [II] | H. E. Scudder | Large Paper".

The regular edition, 2 vols., 12mo, was issued in cloth, back lettered "James | Russell | Lowell | A Biography | I [II] | Horace E. | Scudder | Houghton | Mifflin & Co." The imprint on title is "Boston and New York | Houghton, Mifflin and Company | The Riverside Press. Cambridge | 1901".

Besides numerous extracts from letters, these volumes contain verses here first printed on pp. 38, 46, 54, 68, 73, 75, 77, and 435 of Vol. I, and pp. 47, 75, 116, 215, and 343 of Vol. II.

1902

Early Prose Writings | of | James Russell Lowell | With a Prefatory Note by Dr. Hale, of | Boston, and an Introduction by | Walter Littlefield | [vignette] | Published by John Lane | The Bodley Head | London & New York |

12mo. Collation: Blank, pp. [i–iii]; portrait, title, copyright (dated 1902) and imprint, Contents, Prefatory Note, and Introduction, pp. [iv]–xxxviii; half-title and text, pp. [1]–248. Size of leaf, untrimmed, 7½ by 5¼ inches.

Issued in boards, cloth back, with paper label, "Lowell's | Early | Prose | Writings".

The pieces included in this volume are for the most part reprinted from the *Boston Miscellany*, 1842. One, "Song-writing," appeared first in the *Pioneer*, February, 1843, and had already been printed in the 1873 unauthorized edition of "Conversations on Some of the Old Poets."

The book was printed in New York, and the first edition was issued in September, 1902.

1902

The Anti-Slavery | Papers of | James Russell Lowell | I [II] | [Publishers' device] | Boston and New York | Houghton Mifflin and Company | MDCCCCII

2 vols., 8vo. Collation: Vol. I: Half-title, title, copyright (dated 1902), Introduction, and Contents, pp. [i]–xiii; half-title and text, pp. [1]–223.

Vol. II: Half-title, title, copyright, and Contents, pp. [i]–vii; half-title and text, pp. [1]–203; imprint and number, p. 204. Size of leaf, untrimmed, 9¼ by 5¾ inches.

Issued in boards, with paper label, "Anti- | Slavery | Papers | of | James | Russell | Lowell | I [II]".

The papers included in these volumes originally appeared in the *Pennsylvania Freeman* or the *National Anti-Slavery Standard,* though they are for the most part printed from the original manuscripts. Five hundred copies were printed. The volumes were edited by William Belmont Parker.

"The Complete Writings of James Russell Lowell," Elmwood edition, in sixteen volumes, Boston, 1904, is of interest because of the new letters which appear in Vols. XIV, XV, and XVI. The original two-volume edition of "Letters," published in 1894, was re-edited by Professor Norton, and a considerable number of new letters added, forming three volumes. These three volumes were not published separately from the set. A special edition, called the "Autograph Edition," was printed from the same plates.

1905

James Russell Lowell | His Life and Work | By | Ferris Greenslet | With Illustrations | [device] | Boston and New York | Houghton, Mifflin and Company | The Riverside Press, Cambridge | 1905

12mo. Collation: Half-title, title, copyright (dated 1905), Preface, Contents, and List of Illustrations, pp. [i–xi]; text, and Index, pp. [1]–309; imprint, p. [310]. Frontispiece portrait and illustrations, separately printed, facing pp. 12, 68, 180, 236 and 272. Size of leaf, untrimmed, 7⅜ by 5 inches.

Issued in cloth, back lettered "James | Russell | Lowell | Ferris | Greenslet | Houghton | Mifflin & Co."

This admirable biography includes several letters here first printed and, on pp. 116–121, an extract from an unpublished journal by Lowell.

In Thomas Wentworth's Higginson's "Part of a Man's Life," Boston, 1905, there is separately printed, and facing p. 300, a facsimile of a letter from Lowell to Higginson, dated "Southborough 7th Dec."

1906

Four Poems | The Ballad of the Stranger | King Retro. The Royal Pedi- | gree. and | A Dream I had. By | James Russell Lowell | (Now first collected) | Hingham | Printed for private distribution | The Village Press | 1906

8vo. Collation: Title, Contents, and "Note," pp. [1–5]; text, pp. 7–32; colophon, p. [33]. Size of leaf, untrimmed, 9 by 5¾ inches.

Issued in boards, cloth back, front lettered "Four Poems. | James Russell Lowell."

Two of the four poems in this volume are here printed in book-form for the first time. "King Retro" and "A Dream I had" appeared in the *National Anti-Slavery Standard* for May 10, 1849, and November 28, 1850. "The Royal Pedigree" was first printed, also, in the same paper, but was included in "Poems," 1848. "The Ballad of the Stranger" is here reprinted from "The Token and Atlantic Souvenir," 1842. Fifty copies of the book were printed.

In Elizabeth Robins Pennell's "Life of Charles Godfrey Leland," Boston, 1906, 2 vols., are included letters by Lowell, addressed to Leland, as follows:

Pp. 251–252, extract from letter written in 1861.

Pp. 289–292, letter dated "Elmwood, 16th Oct., 1866." This letter is reproduced in facsimile and inserted between pp. 290 and 291.

Pp. 293–296, letter dated "Elmwood, 9th July, 1867."

INDEX

INDEX

Democracy and other Addresses, 110
Donne (John). Poems, 126
Donne (John). Poetical Works, 44
Dwight (John Sullivan), 128

Early Prose Writings, 130, 131
Emmanuel College, Cambridge. Commemoration of 300th Anniversary, 105
English Poets, The, 115
Essays from the *North American Review*, 95
Everett (A. H.). Poems, 21
Evergreen, 21

Fable for Critics, A, 26, 27, 28, 29, 30, 31, 32
Farrar (Canon). Sir Walter Raleigh and America, 98
Favorite Authors, 57
Fireside Travels, 66
Foreign Relations. *See* Papers Relating to Foreign Relations of the United States
Four Poems, 132
Furnas (R. W.). Arbor Day, 117

Gallery of Mezzotints, 35
Garden Walks with the Poets, 40, 41
Garfield (J. A.), Death of, 96, 97, 98
Garrison (W. L.), Selections from, 41
Gems from the Spirit Mine, 39
Gift, The, 13, 15
Gifts of Genius, 56
Gilder (J. B.). Impressions of Spain, 129
Gill (W. F.). Life of E. A. Poe, 93
Golden Songs of Great Poets, 92
Good Company, 74
Greenslet (Ferris). James Russell Lowell, 131, 132

Hale (E. E.). James Russell Lowell and his Friends, 128, 129
Halleck (F.-G.), Memorial of, 93
Harrison (Gabriel). John Howard Payne, 108
Harvard Book, 87
Harvard Crimson Supplement, 125
Harvard University. Record of Commemoration of 250th Anniversary, 111

Harvardiana, 3, 4
Hawthorne (Julian). Nathaniel Hawthorne and his Wife, 106
Heartsease and Rue, 114, 115
Higginson (H. L.). The Soldier's Field, 120
Higginson (T. W.). Part of a Man's Life, 132
His Imperial Highness the Grand Duke Alexis, 84
History of the Great Western Sanitary Fair, 71
History of the World's Progress, 115, 116
Hughes (T.). True Manliness, 95, 96

Impressions of Spain, 129
Independent in Politics, 113
International Copyright Association, 116

Keats (John). Poetical Works, 42
Kennedy (J. P.), Tributes to, 81, 82
Knickerbocker Gallery, 43, 44
Knight (W.). Wordsworthiana, 105

Ladies' Casket, 22, 23
Landon (M. D.). Kings of the Platform and Pulpit, 122
Last Poems, 126
Latest Literary Essays, 122
Laurel Leaves, 88, 89
Lectures on English Poets, 127
Letters, 124
Liberty Bell, 9, 10, 11, 15, 17, 20, 21, 24, 25, 35, 40
Liberty Chimes, 20
Liberty Minstrel, 16, 17
Library of Tribune Extras, 118
Lines on Reading of the Capture of Fugitive Slaves, 20
Longfellow (H. W.). Poets and Poetry of Europe, 82, 83
Lowell (Maria). Poems, 46
Lowell, Mass. Exercises at 50th Anniversary of Incorporation, 111
Lyman (Theodore, Jr.), Dedication of Fountain in Memory of, 111

Marvell (Andrew). Poetical Works, 47
Mason and Slidell, 59
Masque of Poets, 93, 94

INDEX

INDEX